Biblioasis International Translation Series
General Editor: Stephen Henighan

MOSTARGHIA

MOSTARGHIA

Maya Ombasic

Translated from the French
by Donald Winkler

BIBLIOASIS
Windsor, Ontario

Library and Archives Canada Cataloguing in Publication

Ombasic, Maya
[Mostarghia. English]
Mostarghia / Maya Ombasic ; Donald Winkler, translator.

(Biblioasis international translation series ; no. 27)
Translation of: Mostarghia.
Issued in print and electronic formats.

ISBN 978-1-77196-283-4 (softcover).—ISBN 978-1-77196-284-1 (ebook)

I. Winkler, Donald, translator   II. Title.   III. Title: Mostarghia. English.
IV. Series: Biblioasis international translation series ; no. 27

PS8629.M32M6713   2019   C843'.6   C2018-904462-4
C2018-904463-2

Edited by Stephen Henighan
Copyedited by Emily Donaldson
Cover designed by Natalie Olsen

 Canada Council for the Arts Conseil des Arts du Canada   ONTARIO CREATES | ONTARIO CRÉATIF

 Canada  ONTARIO ARTS COUNCIL CONSEIL DES ARTS DE L'ONTARIO an Ontario government agency un organisme du gouvernement de l'Ontario

Published with the generous assistance of the Canada Council for the Arts, which last year invested $153 million to bring the arts to Canadians throughout the country. Biblioasis also acknowledges the support of the Ontario Arts Council (OAC), an agency of the Government of Ontario, which last year funded 1,709 individual artists and 1,078 organizations in 204 communities across Ontario, for a total of $52.1 million, and the contribution of the Government of Ontario through the Ontario Book Publishing Tax Credit and Ontario Creates. Biblioasis also acknowledges the financial support of the Government of Canada through the National Translation Program for Book Publishing, an initiative of the Roadmap for Canada's Official Languages 2013–2018: Education, Immigration, Communities, for our translation activities.

PRINTED AND BOUND IN CANADA

Mome tati, neutješnom Mostarcu.

I have often wondered what I should do with the rest of my life. Now I know—I shall try and reach Cuba.

— Ernest Hemingway

CONTENTS

BIRTH OF
AN ISLAND

Just a few days before your death you're determined still to be strong, to be the man of the hour, he who can do everything, always, even have his children forget the war and the concentration camps, the bombs and the hunger, the danger and the fear. Your doctor has come to inform us that you are living your last days, and that you are to be moved up to the floor for palliative care. They want to put you on a stretcher to carry you to the floor for the dying, but you refuse. You insist on taking the stairs, leaning, when necessary, on me. I feel you to be short of breath and feverish, like a leaf trembling at the approach of a hurricane. I like your smell, your silky skin, your boniness, and your body's lightness. You were never a big eater, and even before your illness you said we had to feed ourselves like birds, just enough to be able to fly. I see our twin shadows making their way slowly along the hospital corridor. The impassive beauty of the flowers brought to the dying seems extravagant to me in this thankless place. You hold onto me, as once you leaned on my translations in all the countries through which we passed where you refused to learn the language. For a long time I reproached you for this linguistic sulkiness, but towards the end of your life I understood that it was a deliberate strategy, a refusal to accept any social contract. As you lean on me and your breath comes faster, I search for words to tell you how deeply sorry I am for all our misunderstandings. (How to say *sorry* properly in your language, no longer really mine ever since others, like young wives unseating the older ones in a harem, have come to dwell in me, and to make me multiple.) A strange feeling runs through my entire being. As I adjust my body to better serve you as a support, my left breast slips naturally into the cavity in your chest, there where once resided the lung and ribs that have been taken from you. Gently, my breast has begun to swell, to breathe, as if it wanted to become the organ you are lacking, as if it wanted to complete you, but also to hide itself from the world and to return from whence it sprang. At the same time, in a neighbouring room, the Rwandan priest you chased away the other day because he wanted to convert you to Christianity is reading the Bible in a low and solemn voice to someone on the brink of death: "And the Lord God caused a deep sleep to fall upon Adam, and he slept: and he took one of his ribs, and closed up the flesh instead thereof. And the rib, which the Lord God had taken from the man, made he a woman." With your rolling Slavic accent, you whisper in my ear: "My rib is the Adriatic coast. That's where you were conceived. You will conceive in your turn on another coast." Your face, like that of mystics in a trance, glows with a beatific smile, and I have a sudden conviction that you have always understood everything, all the languages and all the codes you claimed not to comprehend.

And so was it by choice that you embraced this silence? To escape men's idiocy, their flawed languages, and their ancient hatreds? Or was it to be true to your vocation as a painter? "There exists in painting," you often said, "an inner light that precedes the ignorance of words, the intellect, and knowledge." Georges de La Tour, your favourite painter, understood that well: the inner light, beyond language, springs from the dark of consciousness. But what to do when faced with the darkness of death? Nothing, ever, will be the same without you, and that mortal ennui I so often experienced in the grey and murky streets of Geneva, will again haunt my nights. As I feel a strange ball forming in the hollow of my throat, like a black hole drawing me more and more into the gloom of early sorrow, I come across a sentence of Charles Juliet's: "To write is to snatch light from the shadows." But writing has always come as an aftermath for me, as if to chew over and digest more fully an event. For the moment I am still trapped inside it, and the very idea of writing seems lazy, idle, indifferent, cowardly. Pending the slow arrival of its lifesaving virtues, I bear witness to your last hours. I am filled with anger. I want to do something. To comfort you. To give you hope. But there is nothing more to do, other than to await your last breath. With each breath you take, I see that empathy has its limits: the greater your suffering, the more I want to flee before this helplessness and that finality. That night I go home to write a letter that I hope to read to you before you disappear. Too late. Mama tells me that it was just before dawn when, your hands upon your stomach, with an air both serene and surprised, you left us. When we reach your bedside, a stilled serenity has taken possession of your face, despite the stiff wind agitating the trees near the hospital. After the official declaration of your death, the doctor tells us that we have an hour to make our farewells. The hour passes in the blink of an eye, and then a white sheet covers your body. Your life's final curtain drops softly into the hollow of your chest. It's there that I want to slide myself—there where you are missing a lung and a few ribs—to keep you company in the morgue. Now orphaned and with no captain for our drifting ship, we go back to the house to think about your funeral. I count my savings, meant to finance a doctorate at the Sorbonne. I only hesitate for a moment: forget Paris! You will rest forever in the land of the sugared trees.

At night, stretched out in your bed, I cannot close my eyes. I think about your short life. You were born on December 28, 1952, in Mostar, the second biggest city in Bosnia-Herzegovina, and one of the sunniest in Europe. That year the Americans, delighted that Tito wasn't allying himself with the Russians, provided military equipment for the Socialist Federal Republic of Yugoslavia. No one suspected these arms were going to be used, forty years on, for us to kill each other. You were born into a communist family where there were already six children, catching your mother by surprise. Forty-six years old when she realized she was three months pregnant, my grandmother had no choice but to keep you. Imagine the look on her face when she was informed you were not arriving alone, and that she had to push harder to enable your brother to see the light of day! The logic of bonding peculiar to twins was crucial in all your relationships. "Only death can separate us," you used to say of your brother. Tito said the same thing about the six republics that comprised the Yugoslav federation. Except the fusion he imposed on his people did not have its origins in a womb, but rather on a continent where, after the fall of the great empires, a new concept supplanted all others: the nation state.

You were twenty-seven years old when I came into the world, and I turned twenty-seven the year of your death. Twenty-seven years entwined in the ruthless grip of intense emotion, typically Slavic, where hatred and love, sadness and burlesque, are knit from the same yarn, as in the films of Emir Kusturica. I tried so often to break out of this pathetic circle. But it's no simple matter for us to free ourselves from the Balkans and their everlasting madness. Your twin brother, devastated since learning the news of your death, badgered me, calling several times a day to make sure that your coffin would be lined not with cotton, but with silk. He exemplifies it well, that Balkan madness. He proved it the day of your funeral, when he decided, as if it were the most natural thing in the world, to throw himself at the coffin and open it in order to satisfy himself that I had followed his orders.

At night I can't close my eyes. I think of the frigid solitude of your body in the morgue, and your legendary claustrophobia. To ship a corpse abroad can sometimes take two weeks. Meanwhile, the only way to get you released from there, your Haitian nurse tells me, is to entrust you to a religious institution that will prepare your body for its final journey. I am caught between your anti-religious principles and the need to spring you from the morgue. I dial the number of the little parish near the hospital.

"Your father is baptized?"

"No, he's a communist . . ."

The priest sends me off to the Department of Foreign Affairs. I explain the situation, and the polite bureaucrat gives me the addresses of churches that "speak your language." The Croatian parish priest asks me for your name.

"What? Your father's called Nenad? I'm sorry, but that sounds Serbian. You have to call the Greek Orthodox pope, or the Armenian."

I call the Greek community centre. The pope speaks Serbo-Croat because his wife comes from Montenegro.

"Your father was called Nenad. . . And your grandfather?"

"Ibrahim."

"I'm sorry, miss, but that's a Muslim name . . ."

Even beyond your death, the labels you wanted nothing to do with know how to follow you around. A Montreal imam is the only cleric who agrees to take care of your body. Two days later, you're transferred to a mosque in Ville Saint-Laurent. They explain to me that men will wash you, cover you in the essential oil of the cypress tree, a symbol of eternity, and that all through this ritual the imam will recite the *suras*, while at the end a collective prayer, *Duhr*, will be dedicated to you. Naively, I assume I will be able to attend both the washing and the prayer. The imam, startled by my ignorance, explains that women are banned from rituals for the dead. Propped against the mosque's wall, I curse religion and its misogynistic leanings while, inside, people are busy preparing your body. Suddenly, the imam, beside himself and furious, comes out of the building:

"You're a liar! Your father is not a Muslim!"

"Of course he is. My grandfather's name was Ibrahim."

"Perhaps he was called Ibrahim, but his son was not circumcised!"

"For us, it wasn't required. We were lay Muslims . . ."

"Then you're not real Muslims."

"No, listen, please take him. I can't go back to square one."

The man throws me a scornful look. Four hours later, I hear his voice intoning a call to prayer, and I approach the mosque. At the main door, a heavyset North African stops me. He has a suburban accent from Marseille. "My sister, come on, what's got into you, my sister? You can't enter here!" He points me the way to the basement, where veiled women huddled in front of a white wall are following, through loudspeakers, the prayers being performed one floor above. Kneeling before the wall, I regret having tarnished your death with religion, you who wanted nothing to do with it.

After the ceremony at the mosque, another takes place at the funeral home that has received the mandate to ship your body overseas. Your coffin is set down at the back of a plain, spare room with a strong odour of lilies. Chamber music provides a background to conversations trying to fill the emptiness. Your coffin is open, and in the room's muted light I make out your face from afar. You seem to be sleeping peacefully, but a primitive fear prevents me from going closer: I can't bear the thought of your being stilled to the end of time. At last, the little girl in me allows herself to howl with pain.

Shepherding your remains, I set foot on the soil of my childhood native land for the first time in fifteen years. I'm torn between sadness and joy, between mourning and my delight in reacquainting myself with the sky, the intoxicating odour of almonds in blossom, the taste of cherries and Turkish delight near the Old Bridge, and, unchanged, the fresh breeze on the Neretva's shores. I have the odd feeling that I'm resuming the normal course of my life, interrupted with no warning by an exploding gas tank. It's as if a hiatus were coming to an end, after all those years spent far from my childhood streets. Your prophecy concerning the place where I will conceive haunts me. I decide to take a trip to the seashore. In the bus going to Split the same feeling of exaltation takes hold of me when, after the arid hills of the Biokovo massif, I make out in the distance the sparkling indigo of the Adriatic Sea. All my childhood memories are tied up with this sea. We so often dreamed of taking to the open water like Robinson Crusoe, of washing up on an island that would be ours. A few summers later we've set sail aboard the ferry *Tiziano*, after our status has altered in the blink of an eye: from carefree tourists, we've been transformed into refugees looked at askance by European democracies. Taking to the open water was practically all we did during those years of exile, and the island and coast of which we had talked so often, telling ourselves this was where we would find our place in the sun, has now become my obsession. It remains for me to take possession of it, and to plumb the mystery of your last words, echoing in my head like a mantra. Just after your funeral, walking in Split's ancient, narrow streets, I come across a new translation of the Bible in a foreign-language bookstore. The back cover states that an ancient error has been corrected: the idea that Eve emerged from Adam's rib, his *côte*, was a misunderstanding. The reading should have been that the woman was beside, *à côté de*, the man, like a cane he would lean on for better or worse. At once I sense we're wrong to think that we choose the settings for our wanderings. It is, rather, they who embrace us, or leave us stranded. The time has come for me to acknowledge that your island prophecies weren't just the incantations of a hermetic poet. Not long after your funeral I feel ready to play my Hemingway card, and to depart for Cuba. But not before setting down the story of our exile.

THE
VALLEY OF
SUGARED TREES

IT ALL STARTED on April 6, 1992. Life is following its normal course: Mama is working and you, you are wavering between your family responsibilities and your desire to escape in order to create. Our house is in Mostar, capital of Herzegovina, the arid region situated between the northern latitudes of mountainous Bosnia and Dalmatia's lapis-lazuli coast. Mostar's praises have been sung by many poets, but it was the Nobel Prize winner Ivo Andrić who knew best how to describe what is special about it: we can never forget its blinding light, which is perturbing to sensitive souls. Seen from on high, the provincial city, with its red roofs, makes one think of Siena or Toulouse, depending on the sun's angle and the reflections on the surrounding hills. Mostar is sliced through by the Neretva, a wild and hurried river that brings freshness to a land where punishing drought and heat almost always have the last word. More importantly, the Neretva's task is to drown past quarrels in the crystalline Adriatic. A serene and carefree joy is afoot in Mostar's streets. No one foresees the tragic turn events are about to take. No one, either, gives any thought to the fact that the very name Bosnia-Herzegovina carries with it the curse of a region that is incurably unstable. Long before the arrival of the Slavs in the seventh century, the ancient Illyrians lived in the Balkan peninsula. The region's hills and mountains are still alive with the muffled echoes of their vanished languages. Bosnia comes from the Illyrian word *boghi*, meaning "which flows," while Herzegovina is derived from the German *herzeg*, duchy. Bosnia-Herzegovina: a duchy that flows . . .

Black cherries. I will forever associate their taste with the last day of my childhood. On that day, astride a cherry-tree branch in the garden of the detestable Emma, an eighty-year-old who loves her orchards more than people, I'm gorging myself on those succulent little fruits and my last sightings of childhood sky. I've just noticed that I've stained my white dress with the stolen purple cherries, when suddenly an enormous explosion shakes the trees, objects, and living things, reducing all the city's windows to an enormous heap of shattered glass. A ghostly silence sets in during the moments that follow. The heavens are obscured by a dense orange cloud, akin to those that herald sand storms. And then the silence is broken by the cries of desperate mothers looking for their children. I've been thrown to the bottom of the cherry tree, and I am still on the ground when I see my mother running to help me. Panicked, she screams out my brother's name. He, unable to grasp the gravity of the situation, is facing, impassive, his "wailing wall," in the cracks of which he's deploying his lizard-hunting expertise. That night on the news we learn that, in front of the military barracks, in the east of the city and not far from our house, someone has exploded a tank of gas. It's the war beginning, but we don't yet know it. After the explosion parents take their children out of school, waiting for the situation to stabilize. But the situation does not stabilize, neither within nor without our lost and panicked little selves, which, like my younger brother's lizards, don't know which way to turn. The band of Roma musicians that came regularly into our neighbourhood, along with their dancing bear, has been replaced by the sound of sirens alerting us to the bomb shelter opening its doors. At first we think it's a joke: World War II is far behind us. Who would attack our great, proud nation?

As curfews are not yet part of our daily life, we spend our evenings eating melons and watermelons on the roof of Uncle Mitcha's house. We have no more obligations—the whole country has come to a standstill—and from this vantage point we admire the strange game playing itself out over our heads. Camped on one of the hills surrounding the city, someone, we don't know who, is firing rockets at the hill across from him (Mostar is encircled by hills, which might explain our climatic and psychological sense of living inside a "boiling pot"). You, you observe the exchange in silence, and I keep asking you to explain the rules to me: "Who are the players?" Casually, you reply, "It doesn't matter who the players are, it's the game that counts." A bomb falls on the house of old Emma, who dies on the spot, which makes all the neighbourhood children happy. Torn to bits, her body spatters the freshly whitewashed walls of her living room. Her daughter, instead of going to the shelter, spends the following months scrubbing at the monstrous stain that refuses to disappear.

We spend almost three months taking advantage of that unforeseen vacation. The night before I turn twelve, a raucous wailing of sirens tears us from our sleep. In the shadowy kitchen I can make out my birthday present wrapped in blue and orange paper. Strangely, Eluard's earth, "blue as an orange," is my favourite French phrase. It's only seventeen years later, when Zehra, our hundred-year-old neighbour, appears before me holding out a crumpled yellowed bag, that I am able to open my present: the complete works of Plato. I don't know who, you or Mama, had the idea of offering them to me, but in time philosophy became my great passion, and then a career that I adore.

That last morning in our house I catch you cursing the people in the city, and their stupid idea of setting off sirens at this ungodly hour. Still, you take along our passports and a few family photos. To get to the shelter we have to cross Emma's orchards. Fortunately, she died in time, otherwise she would certainly have forced us to make a detour, despite the bombs now raining down on the city. We run, and someone, we still don't know who, lands a rocket two metres away from us. When the bomb explodes, Uncle Dragan bounces off the ground like a tennis ball, describes a pirouette in the air, and falls back down like an old rag. This image has never left me. It's the main reason I am unable to take life seriously: from one day to the next, all the adults who intimidated me with their seriousness, their assurance of being unique and indispensable, became babies who, trying to walk, started to cry when they discovered that when you fall, it hurts. I can also trace back to this time your fascination with nuclear-bomb shelters. You insisted on visiting one a few years later when, in Cuba, a hurricane alert forced the inhabitants of a small village, where you regularly went to paint, to take refuge underground.

Inside our shelter in Mostar, we laugh hysterically when Aunt Silvana tells us how Uncle Mitcha left everything up in the air and ran, panicked, into the street, still lathered to the neck, as soon as he heard the sirens. Silvana also shows us her scraped knees, the result of her husband's losing his cool. One day, when he went to fetch his wife at work, the sirens began to whine and Mitcha accelerated abruptly, forgetting that Silvana had only one foot inside the car. She screamed for dear life as her body, like something out of a Western movie, was dragged behind their old, sputtering Lada by her foolish husband.

Curious, I take stock of our new underground life. The fear that dominated my inner self has been replaced by comradeship, the feeling that we're all equals, and that we must, for everyone's good, defuse what is tragic in our situation. While some collapse in laughter, others, like this former air pilot, negotiate with the humanitarian workers who come with medicine, food, and international news. He's concerned about the civil wars that are, according to him, on the verge of breaking out in Africa, a continent he loves and that he has often visited. While outside, bombs are destroying the houses of poor people, we're dying of laughter on learning that Miroslav, our neighbourhood's chimney sweep, attempted suicide the day he learned that he'd won the lottery but that he couldn't claim his enormous winnings from anyone because the Yugoslav federation no longer exists! While Miroslav despairs, his head in his hands, we gorge ourselves on pomegranates, which grow abundantly in Herzegovina's friendly climate. You observe that this year, for the first time, the fruit is bitter, but no one grasps the subtlety of your remark. You're going to spend most of your life in exile painting the pomegranates of your native land. You're going to open our eyes to the bitterness of your favourite fruit, in a valley once called the valley of sugared trees.

Miroslav the chimney sweep is a good friend with whom you used to play checkers and bet on the lottery. Unlike him you were born under a lucky star: three years ago you won a second prize that enabled you to buy a new Golf, a small house, and a motorboat. In the shelter you console Miroslav in your fashion: "It's all right, I'm going to lose everything too, it won't be long." Unlike most of your compatriots, you never caught the European sickness, the sense of being immortal that leads to spending a fortune on a house. Once you'd deposited the lottery cheque, the construction firm specializing in prefabrication set down a magnificent little house on your father's land. Later, when all the houses in the neighbourhood had been destroyed, your little wooden dwelling remained intact, as if it existed in a parallel universe. I attribute this good fortune to your privileged relationship with the Roma. In ex-Yugoslavia, everyone always despised them, except for you and Kusturica. "They're human beings, like you and me. The best way to know a people is to observe how it treats its underclass." Ex-Yugoslavs, however, like most Europeans, regard the Roma as inferior beings. The fascist desire to exterminate them is still given voice in drunkards' taverns, those reliable mirrors of a society's secret thoughts.

It's thanks to your Roma contacts that we'll manage to escape the circle of hell Mostar has become. People think you're crazy to entrust your children to the Roma, but you have complete confidence in them, much more than in the humanitarian workers and the Blue Helmets. You know exactly what you're doing, because no one, ever, would dare fire on a caravan: to kill the Roma is to bring on bad luck for millennia to come. As there's no more room in the last Red Cross convoy taking Bosnian children to the Croat coast, you draw on your talents as a portrait painter to disguise us: holes in our clothes and shoes, soot and charcoal to dirty our cheeks and our naked legs, bows all over our heads. Above all, you tell us to hold our empty hands to the sky, seeking mercy. Mama cries her eyes out when our little faces, pressed to the dirty, fogged window of the caravan, disappear into the distance, perhaps forever. Little brother is frightened by the drunk and toothless characters sleeping, however peacefully, on a bench near his own. A cat purrs at the feet of an old matron trying to braid the hair of her myopic grandchild. The driver is more intent on his radio than on the road. He's listening to the latest news from the madman who's taken over the large Jablanica dam, and who's threatening to blow everything to kingdom come. The maniac is demanding that the transitional government withdraw its forces, and in the name of an ancestor humiliated centuries ago, talks of a land occupied by the *foreigner*. Our caravan heads towards the sea, but nothing ensures we will arrive safe and sound if the madman decides to blow up the dam. It's very hot. The driver is so nervous that the delicate muscle controlling his eyelid is flapping about like a bird without wings. The sweat is running down his forehead, and he can't stop cursing the madman: *"Idiot, idiot!"* Suddenly, little brother kneels in the middle of the caravan and starts praying for the madman to explode the dam. When the old gypsy asks him why he's asking for something so strange, he replies, in all seriousness: "So the big wave will sweep up our house and bring Mama and Papa to us here." The matron looks to the sky and makes the sign of the cross. It's then that I notice the huge Bruce Lee poster glued to the caravan's roof. When I ask her what it is, she replies, quite simply, "He's our God." Our presence seems perfectly normal, no one pays any attention to us, no one asks us anything. We're "the painter's children." As our caravan bears us away from our childhood, I turn over in my head your many visits to the Roma.

I'm seven years old the first time you introduce me to their strange world. As you enter Mostar, near the resort centre of Buna where I spend my time hunting tadpoles, there's a vast plain surrounded by weeping willows. It's there that the Roma live in their tents. They have very little contact with the outside world. It's not because they're particularly solitary: no one's ever been very interested in them, that's all. Their integration into the social fabric has never been a concern for the empires and governments that have succeeded one another in Balkan history. An invisible people, they've always lived on the margins. You know that their isolation and their remote perspective on the world enable them to grasp the repercussions of events long before the official declarations. For you they are a fiercely independent people with an unparalleled lucidity and zest for life. When, in 1984, Sarajevo is selected to host the next Olympic Games, the government decides it must act swiftly to be worthy of the event. It has to quickly do away with "the ugliness" so as not to offend Westerners' sensitive souls. And so you're named "Project Officer for the settlement of the Roma of Herzegovina." You negotiate with the Buna camp "godfather," but you are soon discouraged by his stubbornness. After many fruitless discussions, you decide to execute the government's orders by installing prefabricated houses in the camp. In one week, in place of the old torn tents where entire tribes live, a new "ready-made" neighbourhood appears. But a few days later you find that, inside the prefabricated houses, these dyed-in-the-wool nomads have re-erected their tents and are living as they always have! Responding to indignant journalists appalled by the squandering of public funds, the godfather replies, solemnly, "Our survival depends on our way of life."

Your fascination with the Roma dates from that time. Once the Olympics are over, against the advice of your superiors, you give them permission to destroy the prefabs and to start living as before. That day you become a member of the tribe. You're received as a friend and brother. Your broadness of mind gives you the right to be surrounded by the best musicians and the most beautiful women. As I'm always with you, a Dionysian way of life is revealed to me from a very early age. Just before the start of the war, the camp godfather sends you a note written in reverse, so you have to read it with a mirror because he thinks he's the reincarnation of Leonardo da Vinci: *"Loše se piše tvojoj rasi, spasi pojedinca ako ne možeš pleme."** You have complete faith in their souls' compass, and you come back to the house gloomy and anxious. No one takes you seriously. People laugh when you try to explain to them that something dangerous is being prepared, and that we have to think about saving our skins, even if we can't save the country. Your older brother is angry. Your "childishness" is tarnishing the reputation of the secretary of the Communist Party. "It's insane! What could ever happen to our great federation?" You don't know, but your sixth sense, sharpened by the Roma, incites you to be vigilant. Seeing that nobody is

---

* The bad times are coming; if you cannot save the tribe, save the individual.

listening to you, you decide, to everyone's surprise, to protect "the graves." You leave for the cemetery and you cover your father and grandfather's *mezar* with a layer of concrete. You also clean your great grandmother's grave and add two new layers of concrete to that of your mother. You cut branches of cypress. You plant jasmine on the graves of the women, and lilacs on those of the men. When, later, the bombs destroy everything, including the cemeteries, your lineage will rest in peace, thrice cemented over by your caring hands.

The caravan on which little brother and I are leaving our childhood streets behind gets through the military blockades with no difficulty. We say goodbye to the valley of sugared trees, but also the noise of the bombs. No one has the courage to inspect the caravan, that filthy, confined, suspicious space. When little brother, curious and nonchalant, presses his blond, innocent head to the window overlooking the checkpoint, the shaven-headed soldier speaking to the godfather furrows his brows:

"That blond child, did you steal him from the Catholics or the Muslims?"

The godfather doesn't hesitate.

"From the Muslims!"

"Okay, you can pass."

We reach the Dalmatian coast and come to Split, a city we know like the backs of our hands because before the war we spent all our vacations there. I remember, tears in my eyes, those carefree summers in that city where it was good to be alive. You always loved its architecture. While the godfather looks for a place to park, I lose myself in my memories: every time we visited Split, you sought out the chill shadow of the Diocletian Palace ruins. The residence of the retired Roman emperor, built during the third and fourth centuries, still stood, majestic, at the centre of town. As we walked through the palace ruins, you said over and over that nothing can make men immortal other than the buildings that survive them. We knew the place by heart, and you dreamt of buying an apartment in its residential environs. Wanting to educate me in architecture, you pointed out the temple's features, the hallway, the ramparts, the residences, the mausoleum where Diocletian's remains would lie at rest until the end of time. We left the palace by the Golden Gate to find the huge statue of Gregory of Nin, Bishop of Split, the first clergyman to have asked that Latin be supplanted by Croat in the liturgy. Later, during our years of exile, I was to see in your paintings the austere and commanding silhouette of Gregory sculpted by Ivan Mestrović, with his finger in the air and his golden toe. But the Split we knew no longer exists: a fierce nationalism, like the web of a poisonous spider, has taken it over, isolating it in a soliloquy where every accent other than Croat implies a "Turkish" or "Serbian" threat. A dark cloud has enveloped your country's sky, and mourning, great and small, has become a permanent state for those who are prey to nostalgia, such as yourself. What happened, exactly? Where did it come from, this hatred of differences? Yugoslavia was a huge country, with regions as diverse as the six republics of which it was made up. Apart from the Albanians and the Slovenes, everyone spoke the same language. Then, from one day to the next, in the familiar streets of Split, we had to hide our names and our regional accents.

The godfather "delivers" us to the Red Cross. When we say goodbye, the men stand erect without showing any emotion, and only the old matron weeps: "My children, take care of yourselves, life is hard, very hard. May God be with you at every moment." I burst into tears in my turn, I don't want to exchange their nomad world for that of those fleeing from war. Our names, Mili and Maja, sound Serbian, or perhaps even Turkish. That's why, the humanitarian workers say, we have to rebaptize ourselves Emina and Abdullah, so as not to arouse the suspicions of the other refugees packed like sardines into the former stadium. Veiled women, frightened children, moustachioed husbands, pace like animals in a cage in this space the new Croatian government has provided for them. They have fled the madness of ethnic cleansing in Bosnia. Mama's best friend has lived in Split since completing her medical studies. When she learns of our arrival she hastens to extricate us from an ordeal we will never forget: sleeping crowded together in a huge stadium along with a thousand refugees represents the cruel forfeiture of any concept of modesty or personal space.

We wait for you in Split for eight months. To protect little brother and to spare him the gravity of our situation, I turn myself into the responsible big sister. We go out every day to hunt lizards in the city streets. I go to school. On the handball team I seem to enjoy privileged status, with my accent that is different from that of the other children. But my feeling of superiority does not last. The parents, doubtful of my true identity, order their children to insist I recite the Lord's Prayer by heart. Having grown up in an atheist family, I don't know the prayer. Instead, I recite the famous lines of Desanka Maksimović, who immortalized, in her poem "Krvava Bajka" ("The Tale of Blood"), the barbarism of the Nazis who machine-gunned an entire elementary school in Kragujevac:

Bilo je to u nekoj zemlji seljaka
na brdovitom Balkanu.
umrla je mučeničkom smrću
četa đaka
u jednom danu.

When I recite the poem of the Serbian poetess instead of the Our Father, I suddenly find myself all alone in the middle of the schoolyard. In the days that follow, the children

---

* Once upon a time / at the heart of the mountainous Balkans / a class of students / died as martyrs / in a single day.

continue to spurn me, and even start throwing things at me.
I have to be removed from school. In a purple notebook I
still possess, I write: "Today, I committed the unforgiveable: I
recited a Serbian poem in a Croat schoolyard. But where has
it fled, my mother tongue, Serbo-Croat?" That day, I knew I
was different, and above all I sensed that one day the vocation
of writer would become second nature to me.

It was only years later, walking in the Lovrinac cemetery
in Split, that I grasped the scope of the historical events at the
centre of which, unawares, we found ourselves. In the cemetery, a bit outside the city and surrounded by slender pines,
there are inscribed on an imposing black marble monument
overrun with weeds the names of hundreds of German soldiers who died in Croatia during the Second World War.
Between 1942 and 1945, the ultranationalist Croat government allied itself with the Germans, taking upon itself the
mission of propagating fascism in the Balkans. The Serbs, on
the other hand, mobilized fiercely to resist fascism, along the
way killing hundreds of thousands of Croatian civilians. The
Croats replied with the same results, and so it went, as it has in
the Balkans since the dawn of time. That was barely fifty years
earlier, and now a new war had broken out, whose pretext was
to avenge the memory of those who disappeared. To recite
the words of a Serbian poet in the heart of Catholic Dalmatia
was to rub salt in wounds already reopened by the conflict.
As a young refugee fleeing ethnic cleansing, I had no concept
of how intense those dizzying historical resentments were.

Mama's friend, who is harbouring us, keeps repeating that
everything will soon end, and that we'll be able to go back
home. But to our great distress, we learn that the Croatian-
Bosnian alliance, after successfully repelling the Serbian
attack on the hills overlooking Mostar, has decided to initiate
a new war: Croats against Bosnians. And so, instead of returning to Mostar in a Red Cross convoy, we are sent fifty kilo-

metres from there, to Ljubuški, to grandmother's house. That's where we'll await better days, hoping to see you alive again, you and Mama. Uncle Mitcha and Aunt Silvana take care of us. We sleep curled up together like two orphans. The news confirms the onset of a conflict more serious and probably longer lasting than the first. The two armies tearing each other apart have traced a dividing line that splits our city into West Mostar and East Mostar, with the Neretva serving as a natural frontier. However, before war broke out in this multi-ethnic city, people called themselves, above all, *Mostarci*. Nowhere else have I known a love story so binding between a city and its inhabitants. Is it due to the enchanting climate? To the light that seems to radiate from people and things? Or again, to the mysterious emerald Neretva, which lends a tropical aura to a region that is both dry and hard to reach? This zest for life did not extend beyond the city, not even to its surrounding area. In his desire to urbanize the major centres, did Tito pay too little attention to the outlying regions? Whatever the case, on the Western shores of the Mediterranean and on the other side of the Atlantic Ocean, the experts, when they try to lend meaning to the Yugoslav tragedy, explain the federation's breakdown in terms of economic and territorial conquest under the cover of Western-imposed democratic advances. But in reality, the mentality in the Balkans has evolved so little that the word "crusade" is still as pertinent as ever.

Once a week, thanks to the Red Cross's humanitarian phone line, Mama calls us from a Mostar under siege. When I ask to hear your voice, it's always the same answer: "Papa's working, he'll call you when he can." Meanwhile, Uncle Mitcha has decided to enroll us in school. In the playground the children look at me strangely. My uncle claims it's because I come from the city. Suddenly I spot Marina, a pretty little blonde girl who looks like a porcelain doll, and who attended the same school I did in Mostar. I remember her as a timid young thing who spoke to no one, and who harboured, deep in her eyes, the secret knowledge of true suicides, those capable of leaving this world without thinking twice. In less than a week we become inseparable. I take Marina under my wing and I defend her tooth and nail against all the tribulations that can present themselves to two teenage girls wrenched away from the normal course of life. We soon attract attention, especially from the boys. Our accents and clothes are different, we're prettier and brighter than the other pious little pink-cheeked girls. Aware of this superiority, we assume the air of pharaohs venerated by their people. We do everything together, we wear the same clothes, pronounce words in the same slow and sing-song way, get the same grades, and play the same sports. The only difference is in our taste in boys: Marina is attracted to the daddy's boys who live in the big white houses with remote-controlled shutters imported from Germany, while I go for the reckless ones who behave like unhappy poets.

Our first separation, imposed by the school administration, is a tragedy. The new Minister of Education, a power-hungry autocrat, has decided to introduce mandatory courses in religious orientation and the catechism. Marina ends up in a class with a priest, and I in another where a woman wearing a hijab stands before us, trembling like an autumn leaf. I don't understand what I'm doing in a class where I'm being taught to write in Arabic. I throw the exercise book in the face of the veiled teacher, and I go home in tears, swearing never again to darken the school's doors. Above all, I don't want to be different from the others, and this *new* religion they say is mine is of no interest to me. I just want to find Marina again and to feel like her. Cursing war and religion, "opiate of the people," Uncle Mitcha takes me by the hand and leads me right to the class of Fra Ivan, the priest teaching the catechism to Catholic children. Happy, I take Marina's hand and listen with interest and passion to the story of Jesus's life and death. Fascinated by the personage of Christ, I already love this man who can walk on water and heal the sick. I also like Fra Ivan's stories about his many trips to the Dead Sea, his naps floating on his back in salt water. I love his hands with their long, delicate fingers, his swarthy skin and his smile that radiates goodness. He's intrigued by "*my case*," and I don't understand why. He looks at me with admiration because I'm always first in his class. When I tell him that "it's because I like the story of Jesus," he smiles, despite the sadness in his gaze. Little by little, life resumes its course, but the fact that I was the pupil of the woman in the hijab seems to move the children to look at me strangely. I detect, in the eyes of my former friends, contempt and uneasiness. Marina is loyal. She tries to take my mind off things: "Let them talk, they're peasants." On the news, we see the war becoming ever more destructive. You and Mama are still in Mostar, trapped on the eastern shore. While the other children are doing their homework, we're sitting, mesmerized, in front of the television set: dozens of deaths each day, women being raped systematically, men being led off to the concentration camp.

The international community hardly cares about Mostar. The media, and the eyes of the entire world, are focussed on the barbarity of the ultranationalist Serbs ravaging Sarajevo. "They're going to leave us in peace," Aunt Sylvia believes, because her father, the "grand vizier," has fed, lodged, and employed many of those peasants, has even loaned them many hectares of good land that her son hopes one day to recover. Fra Ivan plays an important role in what's happening. As soon as the survivors return from the front, he tries to lure them to his monastery in Humac to talk to them about the true values of Christ. He says that to kill one's neighbour is to forget the Ten Commandments. But some don't give a whit for heaven or hell, while others, even though they believe in them absolutely, do not regard all men as their neighbours. The more the war intensifies, the more minds narrow. Hooligans launch bombs against mosques that are many centuries old, and at night armed soldiers come looking for the men. "We're not going to do anything to them," they assure their wives and sisters, "we're just going to ask them a few simple questions." Their simple questions last for days, then months, and the men do not return. During that time I dream, like other children my age, of wearing Converse All Star shoes—which Marina owns in all different colours. I dream about it because, secretly, I want to please Josip, a neighbourhood boy two years older than I am, whose nonchalance has beguiled me.

The entire catechism class is preparing to make the pilgrimage to Medjugorje in order to attend the annual celebration of the Virgin's appearance. It's five o'clock in the morning. The suburbs are sleeping while the faithful await a signal from Ivan the priest to begin the pilgrimage. He heads the procession. I am by his side, and we talk philosophy while we walk. He introduces me to the Greeks, to Thomas Aquinas, and Teresa d'Avila. After four and a half hours on the road, he warns me of the bad times to come: "Whatever happens, hunger or persecution, come see me." With the confidence, typical of my age, that nothing can happen to me, I don't much understand what the priest is trying to say. In front of the Church of the Virgin Mary I hear gunfire in the distance. Mostar is thirty kilometres away. I think of Mama and of you. I'd like to be a bird, to fly to you. In the church, the pious celebrate the miracle of the Marian apparitions. Towards the end of the ceremony we all fall into each other's arms. I take the opportunity to go to see Josip and to confess my crush on him. Surprised by my declaration, he leads me into a little alleyway behind the cathedral. There he takes me by the shoulders, pushes me against the wall, and starts to kiss me passionately. Then he utters words that, in my twelve-year-old head, make no sense: "You've pleased me since the first time I saw you. But since my papa is a Bosnian Muslim, and my mother a Croat Catholic, if I go out with you, I'm going to get my whole family in trouble. Everyone will say

I prefer my father's side, and with what's going on, I can't do it. So you have to forget me. Understand?" After this fleeting encounter, he becomes my obsession, all I think about, my reason for living. Perhaps because he presented himself as forbidden fruit. And perhaps also because he taught me that we had something in common: being different.

On our return from Medjugorje, Aunt Silvana tells us that she's lost touch with Mama. She also informs us that she's exhausted all her resources, and that we have nothing more to eat. Curled up on the big bed, my brother and I feel all alone in the world. Suddenly I remember Fra Ivan's words, and I call him. "Come to see me at the monastery right away." In the basement of this imposing building, the priest has set up a little storehouse of food for people in need. Asia sends tons of rice, Italy pasta and sauces, Belgium chocolate and comic books (even if no one understands French or Flemish), France unsold tins of foie gras, Germany sausages and cabbage. As of this first visit, once a week we go to collect our food ration at the Humac monastery. Goran, the father of my friend Marina, is one of the drivers of the convoys reserved for the victims of the war in Bosnia. They arrive by the Adriatic Sea and are unloaded on the Croatian coast, their contents then to be taken to their destination. But as soon as Goran passes through Croatian customs and reaches the territory of West Herzegovina, he heads the convoy towards the yard of his own home. VIP access to the merchandise is reserved for his family. Then come his extended family and the neighbours. What remains, in other words almost nothing, Goran brings to Mostar, to the nerve centre that divides the city in two, there where the Blue Helmets ensure the *democratic process* of the whole affair. Thanks to her father's job, Marina is the best-dressed girl in the region. Her room resembles that of spoiled Hollywood children, it's a Barbie house with stuffed animals reaching to the ceiling. I like going there.

In one of the rare prisoner exchanges, my plump Aunt Amelia returns to us. She's been imprisoned and tortured, but thanks to her best friend's husband, a general in charge of the concentration camp, she was spared the collective rape. We find her confident and apparently little affected by the events. She's a woman of character who quickly takes things in hand. Her outbursts are explosive, and her language is blunt, especially where we are concerned. "Stop whining, you little brats. I don't know where your parents are. Maybe they're alive. Maybe not. We have to keep going!" She's appalled to learn that, while people in Mostar are dying of hunger, the humanitarian convoys destined for the victims of war are ending up in the yards of Croatian truck drivers. One day, Amelia spots Marina, dressed head to toe in brand-name clothes.

"Tell me, sweetheart, where did you get all those clothes?"

"From my papa's work!"

The next day at school, everyone's talking about something scandalous that took place at dawn. A large woman laid herself down on the road used by the convoys. A pistol in her hands, she threatened to kill herself if the driver didn't divert the convoy into her yard. Fearing the consequences if his ruse were discovered, Marina's father complied. And when, in the middle of our yard giving onto the main street, I see a huge mountain of clothes, medicine, food, and stuffed animals, reaching almost to the roof of grandmother's house, for the first time in my life I am overcome by shame. On that day, under a pristine blue sky, what was carefree in me was lost. Only its blue robe of innocence was left behind. I picked it up, this robe. I washed it, scrubbed it, washed it again. To no avail. It still reeked of disillusionment. They say the war began on a different date for everyone; in my child's mind, it began on that day of enormous shame.

Seeing this mountain of clothing and food, I feel that no one will respect me any more, that Josip will abandon me, and that at school everyone will make fun of me. I'm right.

Every new item of clothing I wear provokes taunts from children who shout at me as I pass by: "Donation! Donation!" To regain their respect I decide to share with others the contents of the bags Aunt Amelia has unloaded into our yard. When she learns of my generosity, she slaps me as hard as she can: "So when it's not Goran, it's you stealing from your people? These things are not for our enemies, they've already robbed us enough!" I cry every night, because I don't know how to restore our reputation now that the whole town knows we're refugees and that we're surviving thanks to convoys from abroad. At night we turn out all the lights and lower our voices, so as not to attract more attention to ourselves. Having suddenly become an enemy within, we fear the worst: rape. One moonless night someone knocks rapidly and sharply on the kitchen window. Aunt Silvana is afraid to open it, but when we hear the voice of Ivan the priest she is reassured, opens the door, and throws herself into his arms.

"You have to leave tonight," he tells us. "A driver from the church will come to pick you up around midnight. Be ready, because if you stay here, tomorrow morning you'll be taken to a concentration camp. Ethnic cleansing has been officially declared, and the army has given your house to a family that was driven from their home in central Bosnia."

Silvana dissolves in tears.

"No, it's not possible, it's my parents' house, I was born here, I spent my best years here!"

But the priest insists, and reminds her of the systematic rape of women and young girls. We have an hour to decide what we're going to take with us. Silvana searches through the family albums. She goes into the yard and starts digging a hole, into which she deposits photos and a few valuable objects that belonged to her mother. Little brother doesn't want for anything in the world to lose his box of toys and heroic figures: Batman, Ninja Turtles, and Alf the extraterrestrial. I can't, either, leave behind my diaries with all the details of my adolescence. I call Marina to tell her that we're leaving for the Adriatic coast to visit my mother's best friend, and that we'll be back soon. I also call all my other friends to say goodbye, but no one, their ultranationalist parents repeat, is "available." The priest's car, a Mercedes-Benz, has glided into our yard, behind the mountain of clothes. The driver, a thin young man, has trembling hands and a face scarred with acne. He keeps one eye on us and the other on the head-quarters, and nervously orders us to be quick. After loading us into the car with tinted windows, he passes through the sleeping town at lightning speed, and I see, vanishing behind Herzegovina's serpentine hills, my last days of childhood. The next day, in a room smelling of lavender and regret, I wake up an adult.

We're back in Split. Thirty-two people, from all corners of what has so rapidly ceased to be Yugoslavia, are hidden in this two-room apartment. We're surviving thanks to the mili-tary discipline imposed by our host, a big-hearted woman, a long-time friend of our family. Alone among this herd, where each is trying to resolve his own problems, little brother and I hold tightly to each other. Because of him, I don't have the right to weaken. But one day, when the hubbub of the apart-ment becomes too much for me, I become a little girl again, and at last I weep for my vanished parents. This time it's little brother who consoles me. From the height of his eight years, he repeats to me the words of the old Roma woman: "You must be strong, life is hard, hard, hard."

Desperate, Aunt Silvana decides to call Fra Ivan, but he's "doing his rounds" at the front, and no one knows when he'll be back. One night, late, someone knocks at the door. It's a bearded man, gaunt, with a woman as thin as he is. He can barely stand, and when the door opens completely, he crum-bles to the ground like wax from a candle. I instantly recog-nize my mother's voice, but it's on you that I throw myself with all my strength, at the risk of splintering your weakened

skeleton. As you wrap me in your long, bony arms, I feel at
last that life is beginning again. Fra Ivan has risked his own
life to free you from the hell that Mostar has become. Your
voice is hoarse, and you have trouble talking. As every word
requires a superhuman effort, during the weeks of your convalescence you remain silent. All you want is paper and a few
pencils, to draw. During this time, the thirty-two guardian
angels crowded into the little apartment treat your physical
wounds. No one has access to the other wounds, not even
you. You will never speak about this grotesque period in your
life. The only thing I'll hear you say on the subject is that Ivan
the priest is "a very great man." I detect in your eyes a feeling
of powerlessness, of shame and anger.

This rage you feel towards your own weakness incites
you to heal more quickly. Against all expectations, as soon
as you feel able to walk, you "take things in hand." With
photographs from the war under your arms, you go to the
Red Cross, whose headquarters is located near the Diocletian Palace. Forty-eight hours later we're authorized to leave
Croatian soil. In our single little suitcase we find room for
the drawings that date from your convalescence. In each one
of them I recognize the faces of your Roma friends. We take
the *Tiziano*, the huge ferry that even today links Split with
Ancona in Italy to transport tourists to the destinations of
their dreams. As for us, we don't know where our journey
will end. You look at me sadly, and, like a conquered gladiator,
you lower your head, saying to me softly: "We know where we
started out, but we do not know where or when we are going
to put down anchor."

SAD GENEVA

ABOARD the *Tiziano* it's a curious crowd. There are carefree tourists, and there is us, once just like them, but who now, overnight, have become stateless. We are uneasy, our faces as pale as this cold, grey dawn coming into view on the horizon. For several among us, seasickness has followed homesickness, and the awful smell of vomit is exasperating the Germans returning from vacation. Every refugee has at his feet a little bag, his only tangible remnant of a life that will never return. The conversations are doleful: one among us talks of Tito's strategic errors that resulted in Yugo-slavia's demise; another is convinced that people are pulling strings from outside; yet another says without conviction that he has always wanted to live abroad, and that this compulsory exile is consistent with his deepest desires. We're hungry, and the piece of yellow paper, furnished by the Red Cross to serve as a ticket at the first welcome centre, does not include a meal. We'll have to wait hours, perhaps days, before being entitled to our first bit of charity. You take me by the hand. We go out onto the bridge. The shrill wind blends with the laments of mothers who have lost track of their children in the concen-tration camp. The last star in the sky disappears, and a new day dawns. Your trembling hands try to light a cigarette that the mist instantly dampens.

"As of today, we have neither a country nor a place to live. What's good in all this is that we're as free as air. So what would you like to do later?"

I don't quite understand your question, and I reply automatically:

"Later, I'd like to go back home."

Disarmed, you burst into tears. It's the first time I've seen you cry. It's also the first time I've felt that I have to take care of you. That day, without my realizing it, we switched roles, and I became the captain of our ship.

We dock at Ancona. We're no longer tourists come to shop in Italian stores. We have a new label: *refugees*. Ancona is a town where time has stopped and where the washed-out facades, with their pastels, inspire melancholy. You know we must at all cost avoid places where the soul is easily overwhelmed by waves of sorrow. You cast your eyes over the ancient walls. "Those who want to die of nostalgia, let them stay in this city. It's a place for ghosts from the past." Many of the displaced, however, decide to remain in Ancona. We move on. At the station an officer points out the train for Chiasso, a small Swiss village at the Italian border where a centre welcoming ex-Yugoslav refugees has just opened its doors. Everything seems well organized. The train will even take us right to the centre. We just have to show our paper to the Red Cross, and we'll be accepted at once. We climb aboard a strange, windowless rail car that looks like it's designed for cattle. To our great surprise, we see that it's filled with refugees from all the ports of Italy: Somalis, Rwandans, Congolese, Albanians, and Macedonians, but also with nationals from distant Asian countries. When the sour and acidulous odour of this human throng reaches her nose, Mama bursts into tears. We sit down beside a Congolese family, and little brother immediately befriends a child his age. I shut my eyes to try to flee this suffocating place. A picture keeps coming to my mind: that of a Jewish child being shunted from one train to another before reaching the death camps. Where did I see it, in what militant film? Tito understood well the historical significance of his victory over the Germans, and it's on that foundation that he erected the pillars of Yugoslav unity. Instead of cartoons for children, our little minds were fed with films where brave partisans stood up to the forces of evil.

And while the other passengers try to sleep, despite the lack of air, you look at the ceiling and recite lines from Primo Levi that echo still in my ears:

> *You who live safe*
> *In your warm houses,*
> *You who find, returning in the evening,*
> *Hot food and friendly faces:*
> *Consider if this is a man*
> *Who works in the mud*
> *Who does not know peace,*
> *Who fights for a scrap of bread,*
> *Who dies because of a yes or a no.* *

In Chiasso, a team of doctors and nurses greets us and separates us into two lines: Whites on one side, Asians and Blacks on the other. You light a cigarette, which one of the centre's workers immediately grabs from your hand. Along with others, you try in vain to explain that we are hungry and thirsty. No one listens to you. The atmosphere inside the large tent is oppressive. Like marionettes barely able to stand upright, we throw ourselves on the dry little biscuits handed out by volunteers. There's another sleepless night in the offing, and exhaustion, irritability, and fear are gaining ground. Tears run quietly down the cheeks of both young and old. A bit before dawn,

---

* Translated by Giulio Einaudi

after an extensive medical examination, we collapse onto the
military cots provided for us.

We spend three long months sharing this squalid and
soulless space with a thousand other refugees and emigrants.
You don't comprehend what we're doing there. The days in
Chiasso are long and dull. As we have no right to leave the
premises, all we can do is take refuge in humour, as we did
in the bomb shelters. We laugh at nothing and everything,
especially the racist comments Mama directs at the Africans,
these "savages" she used to see on TV, and with whom she
now spends her days. She's outraged by their barbarous way
of eating with their hands. When Rosette, a hefty Congolese,
rolls a ball of bread in her palms and offers it to Mama as a
mark of friendship, she vomits in her face. It's the declaration
of a sinister racial war.

After Chiasso, we end up at the other end of Switzerland,
in Basel. Your childhood friend, an upright, proud man with a
long, grey mane, a former director of one of the largest Yugo-
slavian oil companies, still loves life. He sometimes disappears for several days to go and sleep under the city's bridges.
He says it makes him feel free again. His eyes gleam with a
light that you often see in crazy people, and which is nothing more than a sign that the limits imposed by norms and
routines are being transcended. War and exile have freed him
from his responsibilities, and he's decided to make the most
of his days. The idea of losing the solace of his friendship is
intolerable to you, so essential has it become in the midst of
this storm that has come to dominate your life. We beg the
Swiss authorities not to separate us from our friends, but they
have no patience with our "childishness." In their eyes we are,
like all Eastern Europeans, a dangerous element, because we
can't control our feelings, and are liable to kill each other at
the drop of a hat. "You people are out of control. You either
adore or detest each other. You're all Karamazov brothers to
the nth degree, so it's best that you be separated," explains

Monsieur Sheller, the chief administrator of the Basel refugee centre, and a former rocker with long hair and dark glasses. What are his criteria for determining people's fate? No one knows.

I often ask myself what sort of adult I would have become had Sheller sent me to Zurich rather than to Geneva. How would I see the world if my adolescent brain had been exposed to German rather than French? Would my poetry's rhythms be different? The taste of mercury in my mouth on nights when I've abandoned hope, would it be the same in the language of Nietzsche as in that of Rousseau? The latter would certainly have had plenty to say about the effects of others' arbitrary choices on our lives. From Basel I retain the hazy memory of Münster, the old cathedral with its pink sandstone walls and slender silhouette. One day I learned that there lies the body of Erasmus, the brilliant Renaissance canon who left us, among other works, his famous *In Praise of Folly*. Had your best friend read it before throwing himself into the liberating arms of unreason?

Then Geneva. In this city that never wanted anything to do with us, I live a solitary adolescence. My only friend is the statue of Jean-Jacques Rousseau on the island that bears his name, planted with weeping willows and Italian poplars to suggest that other island so dear to the philosopher, in the middle of the little lake at Ermenonville. I console myself by thinking that Geneva has always been a bad mother to its children, having closed its doors to Rousseau. Like him, I gave up my Swiss citizenship when the cantonal Population Authority told us that we, the children of refugees, had the right to stay on Swiss soil, but that our parents had to leave because there was no more war in the country of their birth. Meanwhile, like the solitary walker, I am very preoccupied with my soul's salvation. The war cast me into the deeps of human tragedy at an early age, and I am trying to escape by devouring the existentialists. I tell myself that the only way to flee the absurdity of this world is to throw myself into books. I dream of an open-air library in a land where nature would have the last word, far from burdensome memories and lethal identities.

Our first Geneva home is a monastery a few kilometres outside the city. The little commune of Presinge, with a population of barely a thousand, has a school, a church dedicated to Saint Felix, a restaurant, and an abbey, but is of no particular interest other than that it offers whoever has crossed Europe to escape war the opportunity to meditate near the great oaks that grace the main entrance to its monastery. This immense seventeenth-century edifice, converted into a welcome centre for migrants and political refugees, might have been the source of some of our more agreeable Swiss memories. But it will prove to be the opposite. In the eyes of the Swiss authorities we are just Yugoslavs. But Yugoslavia no longer exists, and having to preface our identity with an "ex" leads us, unconsciously, to dwell in the past. I often climb onto the monastery's roof to watch the refugees taking naps on the grass. Seen from above, they seem to be living normal lives. At times they remind me of the nonchalant figures in impressionist paintings, stretched out contentedly in the shade. Close up, it's another story. I'd have liked to be James Ensor, to be able to reproduce the strained faces of the refugees on the grass, and to capture the grotesque tragedy of these empty shells once inhabited by real people. You never painted them.

All the same, during the first days of our stay in Presinge, we're happy to at last have a place to ourselves. After several months sharing everything with others, we now have a real bedroom. It's spacious, and its large windows reaching to the ceiling make us feel like we're living in a Viennese residence. The place is isolated, and surrounded by misty plains that attract hares and foxes. The path leading to the wood is frequented by rich Swiss heirs who indulge in boredom and horseback riding. At times I detect a hint of curiosity in their gaze. Two parallel worlds, that of the uprooted and that of the anchored, rub shoulders every day along the narrow paths of the Geneva countryside. I feel an intense sadness every time I pass a lamplit house that reawakens fond memories.

A school bus takes me every day to the Malagnou school, where I've joined a class designed to welcome refugee children. The Swiss are on one side, the foreigners on another. Later, when I enter Calvin College, I will almost need a petition to be admitted. Only one thing comforts me: Jorge Luis Borges was also one of those rare foreigners to attend this celebrated Geneva college. On the bus to Malagnou, I'm a curiosity for the Swiss children, who mock me, calling me the "mane of fire." I'm not redheaded, but my hair has suddenly gone copper, as if the blaze consuming my country had decided to set alight, as well, my long, heavy tresses. Still, it's a happy autumn. Isabelle Yeu, my French teacher, an extraordinary woman, instils in me a lifelong taste for literature. Frustrated at not being able to read in French, I promise myself to learn as much vocabulary as possible. I first try simple texts such as news reports, and then throw myself, with indescribable pleasure, into the masterpieces of world literature.

The books and the Geneva countryside contribute to the exhilarating happiness of my fourteenth year. Every day, around four o'clock, I take the bus that brings me back to the monastery, where I rejoin you, Mama, and little brother. I'm always first at the bus stop because I'm determined to sit next to a window. While the hormonal din of the Swiss adolescents makes it hard for the driver to concentrate, my gaze absorbs the golden plains. At one with the landscape, I commune with Geneva's wildlife. I'm the hare and I'm the grass. I'm the oak and I'm the fox. I'm the dew and the sunset. I feel a fevered liquid coursing through my veins. Later, reading the mystical biography of Teresa of Ávila, I realize that those moments of exaltation and grace were of a spiritual order difficult to express. All I can now say on the subject that is in any way coherent is, that while I had just lost my country and been torn away from a carefree and happy childhood, and in spite of a father whose needs had suddenly been transformed into those of a man who needed assistance in all his life's initiatives, I experienced a deep oneness with life, a well-being that came close to ecstasy.

But life ran its course, sweeping along in its current sorrows, large and small. With time, my mystical raptures became increasingly rare. To preserve them, I doubtless would have had to isolate myself from the world and to dedicate my life to a spiritual order. But there is nothing mystical about my daily life at Presinge Abbey: an entire community there relies on my services as a translator, and the religion others attribute to me forbids me to worship any god but Allah. However, no one believes, not even the Swiss workers, that we share the same faith as the rest of the Arab world. For Westerners, we're "too white," "too blond," "too educated," to really be Muslim. In fact, we also find this new identity a bit strange. Just yesterday we were Eastern Europeans, Southern Slavs, atheists and socialists, who had never set foot in a mosque, and saw religion as no more than folklore and cultural expression. Were we not all Yugoslavs, with the same language, the same mentality, the same Latin and Slav soul, with here and there a few genes and traditions derived from the Turks who came to colonize these lands in the wake of Ottoman conquests? Now, though, with the disintegration of the Yugoslav federation, we had lost this identity, which we thought to be immutable.

The awakening is brutal. How to face up to the fact that history has once again dealt us a rotten hand? The peoples of the Balkans have always been crash-test dummies. A crossroads between West and East, between Catholicism and the Orthodox Church, between Christianity and Islam, between tradition and modernity, the peninsula still boasts remnants of all the empires that formed it: Greek, Roman, Ottoman,

Austro-Hungarian. The bright side of these conquered territories' overly violent past is to be found in a cosmopolitan ambiance that was nowhere so vibrant as in their urban centres: Babylon, Carthage, Alexandria, Cordova, Salonika, Istanbul, Beirut, Sarajevo. And yet "civilized Europe" allowed the very idea of a cultural mix and multiple identities to wither away in Sarajevo and in Mostar. Those who come from these cities are cursed with an indelible memory of a time when a zest for life, over and above all the constraints associated with identity, represented the most natural way of being in the world.

The other refugees staying at the Presinge monastery come from the same country that we did, but they know nothing of Mostar. For you, that's almost an insult. "But where have you been living all these years? You've never set foot in Mostar?" For you, to be born in Mostar means many things. Understanding the language of poets, speaking it with a musical accent, instantly recognizable, sipping a *rakija* in the shadow of fig trees leaning over the turbulent Neretva, eating *ćevapi*, our national kebab, in the old city, with its air of Istanbul, being ready to give one's life for our football club, stuffing ourselves with roasted chestnuts sold by the Roma in autumn, making a *méchoui* on the first of May, eating freshly caught eel, being intoxicated by the perfume of the cherry and almond trees flowering in springtime, jumping from the old bridge, arms spread wide, head first into the Neretva, feeding turtles in the schoolyard, tossing pomegranates that look like blood when they burst, drying apricot pits in the sun, threading tobacco leaves in the plantations where you find the shambling, languid silhouettes of old men who once fought fascism, tasting nonchalance in a Turkish coffee, knowing how to recite by heart the exploits of the partisans and visiting the "strategic sites" of battles against the Germans, raising a statue to Bruce Lee and launching ourselves into the rapids on inner tubes to go and buy an ice cream from the Albanian who found his lucky star in our city.

The question, "What religion are you?," frequently asked by our countrymen, disgusts you. And you almost want to get into a fight with them when you realize, despairingly, that not only have they never seen your city, but that it leaves them utterly indifferent. You don't know how to explain to them that the question of religion is out of date, irrelevant since Tito gave us a nationality. You don't know how to make these peasants understand that just being in Mostar is enough to make you feel like a citizen of the world, once and for all. The Stari Most, the *old bridge* that gave its name to the city, incorporated in its five-hundred-year-old stones its inhabitants' large and small differences in the name of something vaster, seeming to defy the laws of physics. This sixteenth-century marvel's perfect arch, designed by the architect Suleiman the Magnificent, allowed ideas to rise into the air and to transform themselves into eternal dreams. As for the hotheads burned by the sun, they could jump into the icy Neretva, which refreshed both body and mind. In this cosmopolitan city where religion never threw up a barrier between people, you could call yourself Igor or Vesna and still be a Muslim.

You're deeply saddened to find that the mentality of people from the same country as you is as remote as that of the Congolese, who are trying to teach us Lingala. But you try to understand their ignorance, and you talk at length about the living conditions of peasants in our country. "It's true that they're badly treated, just like the poor and excluded all over the world." To prove your point you bring out your bedside reading, *Christ Stopped at Eboli*, by Carlo Levi: "This passive brotherhood, this common suffering, this resigned, united, and secular patience, is the deep feeling that holds the peasants together, a bond not religious, but natural." You have also given yourself the mission to educate those peasants. Every night, in the large hall that serves as a meeting room, migrants from various nations gather around their leader. We understand nothing of the Africans' passionate debates, even less of discussions among the Asians, which seem more like quarrels. You, seated in the midst of the ex-Yugoslavs, deliver speeches that can last for hours:

"From a purely geographical point of view, civilization had a hard time forging a path through the mountainous landscape of the Balkans. The rude and arid panoramas, with sharp, exposed stone on every side, inhibited one's gaze from carrying far towards the infinite—despite frequent apparitions of the Virgin. This complex geology, produced by the junction between the African and Eurasian tectonic plates, throws up inaccessible rocks and hills that create natural frontiers between one village and another, sometimes over a distance of twenty kilometres . . ."

Mama looks askance at your public speaking and the leader status you've accorded yourself. She knows better than you the peasants' mentality, and she knows that your desire to enlighten them could backfire. You pay no heed to her warnings, you think we are "among our own," that we must do everything we can to educate them. But the peasants themselves whisper in the corridors that you are a Serbian spy, perhaps even a war criminal in disguise. At first, you pay no heed to these absurdities. And then you start declaring that no event, not even a war, can open narrow minds: futile then to try to educate them. Frustrated, you mumble into your beard: "Man is made up of the least malleable stone there is: from birth to death, our journey on earth carries with it the same limited reservoir of thoughts, with here and there a few variations."

The tension mounts. We are seen as a threat, even if you repeat that your father's name was Ibrahim, that your grandfather was a Turkish settler, but that you, you're not a believer. The mistrust goes up a notch with the regular visits of a Syrian journalist whom we met by chance during one of those meaningless visits from international organizations. Hosting those outings are among the responsibilities of the social workers dealing with our case. The workers show us off to UN representatives who have come to marvel, as when Europeans installed American Indians in their museums, at the re-emergence of a species: the Balkan war refugee. Derviche is a journalist who works for an organization with a humanitarian mission. Shortly after having met us he decides to pay us visits on a regular basis, citing his connection with a certain religious brotherhood. Those visits sometimes last three days, until Mama realizes that he's sexually aroused when I am near him, and that the true purpose of his solicitude is to increase the number of concubines he is amassing as trophies in his Damascus harem. If the other refugees look on his visits with disapproval, it's mainly because the journalist is implying that he belongs to a royal family, and they think we're profiting from his millions. "Why is he cozying up to a Serbian family instead of helping us poor Bosnians?" ask those for whom we are anything but "true Bosnians." The real injustice is rather that the Syrian raids our refrigerator, stuffing himself with "authentic Bosnian cuisine."

While we are mourning a nationality and a country, we must at every moment justify our existence in order to avoid violence. The peasants are stubborn, and for them anything is permitted, including rape, which I escape by the skin of my teeth. Our first names are enough to kindle the hatred that besets us. To survive in this hostile place, we draw closer to the Somalis and the Congolese. Your son, Mili, becomes the best friend of Alexandre, a little Congolese who dreams of becoming the new Pelé. After six months, instead of learning French, Mili speaks fluent Lingala. According to Alexandre's parents, fair-haired little brother has become an expert in Lingala insults: "*Na go beta you mami!*"* Mama worries a little about her son's liking for Congolese cuisine, especially a strange specialty, the earthworm sandwich. Days pass, and

---

* I'm going to hit you, Mama!

we are more and more isolated. No one talks to us, paranoia is
on the increase, and our most hardened enemies try to incite
the social workers against us. To lower the tension, we are
transferred to a centre on the other side of Geneva, not far
from the airport, populated mostly by Bulgarians, Albanians,
and Africans. We have two rooms, with a common kitchen
and shared toilet. Things go a bit better, but every night we
are awakened by the cries of an old Afghan woman, blind
and mad, whom Russian soldiers raped in the presence of
her husband before killing him in front of her eyes. The old
woman starts screaming every time she hears us talk because,
for her, we are Russian. At night she comes banging at our
door to curse us in her language, which we don't understand.
How to explain that we are political refugees, just like her?
Her cries have become so unbearable for everyone that the
Swiss authorities decide to remove us from the hostility
we continue to inspire on every side because of our patent
hybridity.

The Geneva canton's General Hospice gives us enough
support to pay for a decent apartment. Mama, with the help
of our social assistant, finds one in the centre of Geneva, near
Cornavin station. The thought of being at last in our own
home delights us. The lodging, on the first floor of a cement
building, has three bedrooms and a large kitchen, not counting the balcony you intend to use to store your paintings.
But the day we are to move in the owner calls to tell us that
the apartment is no longer available because a woman from
Sarajevo, who has just lost her husband to sniper fire, has pri-
ority over us. He shows us another apartment. Situated on
the building's top floor, it's a studio into which are crowded
the shower, the basin, the bed, and the clothes washer. We
accept without thinking. That night will be the worst since
our arrival in Switzerland. The room is infested with cockroaches that assail us from all sides. In the small room where
the four of us sleep you exterminate fifty of those horrible

bugs that taxi across our bodies like planes at a busy airport. Exasperated, you go into the street to find a piece of cardboard, on which you draw a family in a roofless house. You write underneath: REFUGEES FROM WAR, VICTIMS OF DISCRIMINATION, WE SEEK A SHELTER, PREFERABLY WITHOUT COCKROACHES OR SMALL MINDS.

With two suitcases holding all our possessions, we go down into the street, where grace and mercy await us. Journalists plead our cause and the Swiss authorities rapidly take matters in hand so Geneva, that Mecca for international organizations, won't be shamed by the spectacle of a family of refugees in the street. Things move quickly, and for the first time since the beginning of the war we have a decent place to live. We'll spend seven long years in this apartment on the rue de la Servette. The money the city gives us barely covers our rent, and we also have to eat. You sell a few canvases, but that's not enough for us to survive. At this time, the Swiss franc is four times as strong as the French, and many Swiss go to France to shop. We have no other choice but to break the law by crossing the border in secret. With the cross-border workers at Malagnou, we melt into the morning crowd and cross the border on foot. We spend the day at Annemasse, where we fill our bags with cheese, meat, eggs, bread, delicatessen products, vegetables, fruits, and sweets as well, for days when we have the blues. We scrape by like that until Mama is hired as a chambermaid in a hotel on the rue de Berne. I wait for my next birthday to be able to work in the same luxury hotel, designed to impress the Saudis.

The fact is that every year, from June to August, Geneva is overrun by rich Saudis. The Swiss ridicule them, but their presence on Swiss soil greatly enhances the national economy, and hypocrisy is very much alive when the banks can profit. I clean the rooms on the seventh floor of the hotel, where every year a prince and his eleven wives take up residence. He sleeps alone in the large suite at the end of the corridor, and certain evenings treats himself to Moroccan and Tunisian high-end prostitutes, each more beautiful than the last. During the day, the sheik visits his wives, and takes siestas with each of them. One day, while I am changing the sheets of his enormous royal bed covered with piles of silk pillows, I sense a presence behind me. The man is tall and elegant; with his long white tunic and his hair held in place with a golden cord, he's like a vision. His wide black eyes burn with desire for my youth. He asks me in English: "Beautiful stranger, where do you come from?" Without waiting for an answer, he approaches and strokes my face. Covered in perspiration, I am as still as a sphinx. "Your beauty is the one piece lacking from my harem. Be my precious stone. Be my Achilles heel."

The prince has an erection. His tunic resembles Mont Blanc. But the door is open, and I hear the footsteps of Christine, the governess. She enters the room, scolding me:

"Didn't I tell you not to come in when someone is in the room!"

The prince turns to her, indignant.

"Who permitted you to talk like that? This is my sister, and perhaps my promised one, if she accepts to be my wife!"

Christine is frozen in place. She doesn't know how to react. The man picks up his Versace glasses, which are sitting beside his many perfumes, and leaves the room. Christine hops around me like a headless chicken. "You're going to be a princess! A princess!" Mama, who's working on the same floor, also enters the room. When Christine describes the scene, she starts to weep with anger. In her awkward French, she puts the Swiss woman in her place:

"My daughter will marry no prince. I didn't save her from the war so she could become a concubine. She's going to study and become a businesswoman. She's going to take your place!"

Mama drags me out of the room and orders me back to the house. But the affair doesn't end there. The prince has summoned the hotel management and my mother to a private meeting. He has also asked that you be given an invitation, but obviously, no stranger to your temperament, Mama has been careful not to do so, knowing full well that you would be capable, for your daughter, of converting the prince into a Yugoslav shish kebab. I go with Mama to the meeting, to translate the proceedings from English to French. Mama firmly refuses an offer of a million dollars, and politely asks the prince to leave her family in peace. He doesn't understand.

"You prefer to see your daughter dressed like a slave when she could be wearing royal robes?"

Mama stares him down. She turns briefly to me, ordering me to translate her reply without omitting a single word.

"I prefer to see my daughter dressed as a child! The war took her toys out of her hands, and no prince will ever be able to give her back her childhood innocence. Leave her alone so she may become an adult at her own speed."

That night I am subjected to my first ever bargaining session. "No is no!" repeats Mama in desperation to the hotel management, who could have pocketed a pretty sum. But things are going to become even more complicated. Other Bosnians working at the hotel are convinced that we're Serbs passing as Muslims to curry favour with the rich Arab princes that they themselves dream of wooing every day of their lives. Their jealousy is such that they denounce us for working as illegals. Three days later Mama and I are summoned to the office of our social worker, a rigid woman from Quebec, married to a Swiss. Sitting stiffly on her chair, she announces our fall from grace: we lose our social assistance, and the money we've earned illegally, some twenty thousand Swiss francs, must be reimbursed immediately. Mama is shattered. "Please, Madame . . ." The woman from Quebec is unbending: twenty thousand francs must be returned to the City of Geneva within thirty days, or she will demand our extradition. Mama returns home defeated and decides to tell all. Furious, you blame everything on "the Arabs." "All our problems are caused by them. Yesterday, it was the bloody Syrian who came to empty our refrigerator and rub up against our daughter while calling me 'my brother,' and now it's that Saudi who wants to buy her!"

You light a cigarette and pour yourself another beer, keeping an eye on the small screen where your horse is galloping. Lately you've been betting on the races at the Swiss hippodrome. You think it's the only way for us to get out of this bind. Monitoring Number 8, your favourite, you continue to rant. "This shitty prince thinks he's king of the world? Why didn't you call me? I would have buried a Yugoslav sword in his belly! When I think that Europe hates us because it thinks we're related to them!" We don't know how to calm him down. "We have to separate Islam from the Saudis, prove to the world that we're different, that our Islam is a recent business that dates from the Turkish colonization, and that we don't want to be like them! Otherwise, they'll take us for fanatics. Bad times are on their way . . ."

During our entire stay in Switzerland, you wanted to demonstrate that Bosnians are not like other Muslims, that we are Christian heretics converted to Islam, and that the misfortune afflicting us today is but an extension of the massacre of the heretics in medieval Europe. Shut up in your studio, you paint raw, famished faces, tortured corpses, fearful gazes, but also steles and crosses with half-Byzantine, half-Egyptian symbols. You were always fascinated by the Bosnian heresy from the Middle Ages. "In Bosnia's past you find the shared history that enables us to understand the present, and to save our land from the darkness of segregation." You try to explain to your own people that Bosnia's history did not begin with the Ottoman Empire, that you have to go back to the schism of 1054, which divided Christianity between Rome and Constantinople, and then to the twelfth century, when the Bogomils, believers in a Christian and Manichean heresy born in Bulgaria, refused to follow the Pope. Some even claim that Martin Luther, several centuries later, came to visit them before laying the foundations of his new heresy: Protestantism.

But your "godless" paintings and sculptures, and your theories on the heretic, Christian, and Orthodox origins of our ancestors, just confirm in the minds of Geneva's Bosnian Muslim refugees that you're a Serbian criminal who is pretending to be one of theirs. You ignore their threats and continue to work away with missionary zeal. Meanwhile, the ravages of war and the concentration camps run riot in your land. Almost every day you lose someone you knew "very well." On the one hand you strive to "rescue your people" from the jaws of ignorance, while on the other you try to persuade civilized Europe that its silence before the Bosnian genocide is the same as that which reigned during the Cathar massacre and the other persecutions devolving from papist fanaticism.

Every time our itinerary permits it, we stop at the Parc des Bastions. You like to play chess with the other immigrants, while I sit down to read in peace. With one ear I hear you complaining about the Baudelairean spleen that's tormenting you in Switzerland, while simultaneously I try to understand why Charles Ramuz is considered the greatest Swiss writer. But your words seep into my reading, and from high in your tragically Slav pulpit, I hear you preaching in your language to the Portuguese and Italians: "This land is boring. It hasn't known war for eight centuries. That's why the Swiss are so good at watchmaking. It's easy to master the mechanism of watches when time does not exist. The only thing that could upset these people would be if a mountain fell on them." The old men look at you with wonder; they don't understand what you're talking about, but the gleam in their eyes tells me that they catch the meaning of your words through your tragic voice. As you utter them, I'm immersed in *Derborence*, one of Ramuz's masterpieces. Suddenly, I read the following sentence: "It's the mountain that fell." Derborence is a place far back in the canton of Valais where, in 1714, a mountain crumbled, killing the twenty or so people who lived at its feet. The event was so rare in the stable and eventless life of the Swiss that Ramuz made a novel out of it that lent his name to posterity.

Our years in Switzerland proceed like a slow dwindling away. You drown yourself more and more in alcohol until the diagnosis comes down: you have to go for a cure in a detox centre. You refuse. They insist. You resist. You're dragged off in handcuffs, for your own good. I observe all this with tired eyes. I have no more fight left in me, and so every day seems to lead to some new tragedy. You leave the centre on December 14, 1995, the day the Dayton Accords are signed. The war is over, despite the aberration of Bosnia-Herzegovina being split up to form a new federation and a functioning country with three founding peoples: Serb, Croat, and Bosnian, each with their own territorial identity and dream of independence. In short, the problems of the Yugoslav federation are passed on to the territory of Bosnia-Herzegovina.

For the Swiss, our war is over, and we can now return. The Population Authority informs us of its decision: the children can remain on Swiss soil, but not their parents. This baffling verdict, and the persecution to which we are being subjected in our own community, has us shifting our gaze towards the American continent. But you are thinking, rather, of a return to our country. We must go back one day, to help it rebuild! And then you learn that your brother Slobodan, the gentle, retired old man, was savagely beaten by four young Croats who don't even know why, really, they assailed him with blows. After emerging from a coma that lasted three long weeks, my uncle surprised everyone, including the mother of one of his attackers, who came to beg forgiveness for her son, by quoting Christ: "Forgive them, for they know not what they do." Despite this drama, you do not change your mind, because you're as stubborn as a mule. One of your best friends, who calls you from Zurich, tries to reason with you:

"You can't take your children into a country with no laws, where for no reason at all they can lose their lives!"

But you don't want to listen, and to justify yourself you resort to this sentence that has become legendary for us all:

"Exile, survival, struggle—that wears you down, it squanders your life force."

RETURNING THE BETTER TO LEAVE AGAIN

W e've decided to go back. You've bought an old Ford in which we cross Switzerland and Italy to reach Ancona. The ferry from our first exile is waiting there for us, to make the crossing in the opposite direction. When you see the huge iron machine, you are filled with a euphoria that must be not unlike that of Ulysses when he spotted Ithaca. Like a child who doesn't know how to contain his joy, you jump from one passerby to the next, repeating to whoever wants to listen: "We're on our way home!" We watch you impassively, appalled by your obliviousness: as if all were for the best in the best of all worlds, as if we still had our house waiting for us, and as if we were just going to pick up the threads of our life where we had left them! Mama whispers softly in my ear: "Whoever marries a poet is certain never to have a roof."

But you start to come back down to earth as soon as we leave the Dalmatian coast and move into the hilly zones of the Balkans, where every ethnic group thinks it has right on its side. The signs, the graffiti, and the slogans are an eloquent reflection of how things stand. From one town to another, the religious and political allegiances flaunt their warring colours. Each preaches for its own parish, and all are fanatical. You dread the return to Mostar, and you decide not to face it right away. You fear your own emotions, and the reunions with those you knew. You take us instead to Sarajevo. When you discover a city in ruins, where every wall shows signs of bullets and blood, your hands start to tremble and you lose your sense of direction. You don't understand how so much barbarity could be inflicted on a single city. The images we saw from Switzerland did not do justice to the scope of the destruction. Sarajevo, the ancient mixed-blood beauty, with its Ottoman and Austro-Hungarian architecture, is no more than a phantom city where the odour of death works its way right into your clothes. For almost ten years, you say, Europeans watched the barbarous and gratuitous spectacle of the tragedy taking place on the territory of the former Yugoslav Socialist Federation. Looking for landmarks to orient yourself in the city you once knew by heart, you curse all those who, taken by surprise, are still wondering how to react and what to think of this conflict, shifting their position from that of eager voyeur to one of passive witness. They did not react when they saw cities being besieged before their incredulous eyes: Vukovar, Dubrovnik, Sarajevo, Mostar, Goražde, Žepa, Srebrenica. . . This procession left them dumbfounded, because they had not learned how to react to such wanton evil. To your mind, they have a poor knowledge of history because behind the Balkans there is Greece, the cradle of tragedy. Some call the Balkans "Europe's Asia." They can't even say where exactly it begins: in Vienna, in Zagreb, in Belgrade, or in Sarajevo? It all depends, you say, on the observer. The Viennese shift the frontier towards the Croats, who push it to the Serbs, and so on. The one thing certain in these lands is that everything has been in flux since the beginning, the empires, the borders, the mentalities, the hopes.

Still wandering through the city's streets, you continue your monologue: "The ancient Greeks gave us a lesson in humility. They said everything, did everything, created everything, thought everything. Plato, the enlightened, entered into every layer of the individual and collective soul. His master, Socrates, revealed the absolute and universal ignorance of ordinary mortals in their relationship to the world and to themselves. But the great Aeschylus showed us that, since the dawn of time, in that part of the world, everything comes down to protagonists confronting each other, key figures who negotiate agreements and declare wars while innocents pay the price with their blood. Culture, once again, has not succeeded in extinguishing the fires of hatred, despite two thousand years of an apparent triumph of reason over myth. And for the umpteenth time, Europe has seen madness erupt from the cradle of civilization: one more tragedy that confounds family histories with history itself. Nothing new in the garden of eternal return, always the same. Those who orchestrated this war harboured in their very genes the traces of past tragedies and hatreds: the father of the Serbian president Milošević blew his brains out. His mother and uncle were hanged. The father of the Croatian president Tudjman committed suicide after killing his wife. The daughter of the criminal general Mladić, Ana, also killed herself because of an obscure family intrigue. The father of the most famous butcher of the war, Radovan Karadžić, he who orchestrated the siege of Sarajevo, raped a minor and had to suffer the consequences. As for the family of President Izetbegović, we know nothing for the moment, because, being Muslim, his line is pure and untouchable, in the image of its prophet. All peoples' tragedies have their origins in family histories."

Mama is tired of turning in circles and hearing you bemoan your fate. She begs you to stop the car and to ask for help from a passerby. But your pride won't allow this. Instead, you remind us of the shooting of the film *Peaceful Days in Sarajevo*. You think you recognize the street where most of the scenes were shot. "Nenad, please, we're not in a film. I want to go and see my niece!" The niece has just given birth. But you don't listen to your wife, and you keep on talking:

"The Young French director came to Sarajevo in the middle of the war, to film its reality; the actors played themselves. You have to admire his courage: few foreign artists would have risked their lives in that way. I especially like the almost total absence of dialogue in his film: the silence of the damaged bodies is enough to communicate what cannot be expressed. He understood well that you have to beware of words when it's a question of evil. To give voice to evil is often to justify it. Language has its murderous mechanisms— that should no longer be a surprise to anyone! Prominent intellectuals have, for example, used the word 'essence' to set entire populations at each other's throats. Now where there is essence, there is also non-being, the reduction to nothingness of all that is not part of this essence. The vocabulary of propaganda has ravaged cities and brought down monuments: churches, mosques, palaces, monasteries, ancient steles, bridges. Words have even attacked their own dwelling place: the Vijećnica library possessed, before its deliberate and barbarous destruction, some of the Balkans', and humanity's, most beautiful treasures. Only a few illuminated manuscripts and irreplaceable incunabula have survived. The Serbs cut off the water to prevent the populace from putting out the blaze, and snipers fired on those who tried to save the books. A few days later, the cellist Smailović played in the ruins of the library, just as he had done, twenty-two days in a row, in the crater left by the Serb shell that had killed twenty-two civilian victims." After the assault of savagery upon culture, culture as a bulwark against savagery . . .

Seeing your country ravaged by an ancient hatred, you repeat, as you drive, that only culture and education can free poor people from the vicious circle of warlike visionary beliefs, whether inspired by Christ or Allah, of nation or race. They must distance themselves from the illusory demands based on identity, refuse to let themselves be manipulated by the marketing of nationalists, and, above all, become aware that a thirst for grandeur is a personality disorder of Balkan man, this troubled being who doesn't know how to accept his smallness and his finitude. You hide behind this monologue so as not to succumb to your emotions. We want to stop to see our Sarajevo cousins, to get their news. But you refuse because you want to get to Mostar as fast as you can.

Once we have passed through the tunnel that symbolically separates Bosnia and Herzegovina, your hands begin to tremble. We don't know how to read the emotion on your face. You decide that, before anything else, we're going to see our house. You don't yet know that one of your childhood friends has occupied it with his family. When his little boy learns that we're the owners, he grabs your leg, sobbing, and begs you not to throw him out. Surprised by their presence, but also by the deplorable state of the house, you want to leave them in peace. Mama is angry. She doesn't know how or why she's gone along with your madness and returned to this country. "And us? Where are we going to sleep tonight?" You lower your head and whisper: "Please . . . I don't have the heart to tell them to leave." In the end we spend two weeks with the wife of one of your good friends, who died a few years earlier.

In this city now populated by widows and orphans, the women, who must alone answer to the needs of their offspring, have become iron ladies. I knew Jasna before the war, when I was seven. At the time, Mama was looking desperately for a babysitter to watch after little brother while I was just starting school. Pregnant with her second child, Jasna was having a hard time finding a real job and was looking for extra money. With her golden hair and Greek goddess profile, she at times resembled Dalida. Dragan, her husband, was tall and well built, and had swarthy skin and a smile that would have appealed to the painters of the Novecento. All the neighbourhood women dreamed of him, including the young girls just discovering their sexuality. (I would realize much later that my masculine ideal much resembles him; tall, dark, deep-voiced.)

Dragan had an air of Sylvester Stallone, and every time they saw the couple, the neighbourhood gossips smirked and called them Dalida and Rocky. Hopelessly in love with his wife, the mechanic assented to all her whims. During the first years of their marriage, they lived in a rented house, but Jasna spent her time cutting photos of luxurious villas out of German magazines. She dreamed of a spacious dwelling with three floors, a swimming pool on the roof, and another in the garden, and also an Audi convertible. Despite his decent salary—he was the most respected mechanic in Mostar—Dragan couldn't satisfy the material expectations of Jasna, who insulted him because he refused to emigrate to Germany. Deep inside, she knew she could do anything with him, except force him to leave his native city. Dragan suffered, like many other inhabitants of the city, from the very real affliction, never diagnosed, that I called *mostarghia*. Jasna was well placed to recognize it, since, being a nurse, she'd dealt with many such cases.

It was in this hospital environment that she claimed to have met the future wife of Muammar Gaddafi during the 1960s. Safia, whose Bosnian and Catholic origins were, according to Jasna, carefully concealed by the Libyan regime, became the colonel's second wife, and she gave him six sons. Jasna had fond memories of this determined woman with whom she had quickly become fast friends. Both dreamed of a better future, and together made plans for grandiose marriages with men who would make their mark on history. The dream became a reality for Safia: in marrying Gaddafi, whom she met when he was studying aeronautics in Mostar, she became Libya's first lady, but Jasna had to reconcile herself to escaping into magazines and looking for a dream house while complaining about a life that was too banal for her tastes. Even today, whenever she's reminded that Gaddafi was a terrible dictator who, had he survived his fall, would have had to answer for his acts, Jasna laughs out loud and repeats, "Once a queen, always a queen!"

Bitter as the wild almond tree that grows by the side of her swimming pool, she lights one cigarette after another as she talks about the war's beginnings. Despite the pressure exerted by his family members who emigrated to the United States when the war started, Dragan never wanted to leave his native city. Jasna would have liked to remake her life on the other side of the Atlantic, but, seeing that her husband refused *"ko magarac"* (like a donkey) to leave Mostar, she promised herself she would make him pay for his stubbornness. Dragan was a peaceable person who would never have imagined taking up arms one day. But Jasna forced him to join the army to defend his city, "since he loved it so much." Dragan discovered that he had a gift for soldiering, and was soon promoted to the rank of general. He was wounded several times, but Jasna, still the good nurse, took excellent care of his damaged limbs, got him on his feet as rapidly as possible, and sent him back to the front. "You wanted a war? You've got it!"

Knowing that we've come from afar and that she is an object of malicious gossip, Jasna, who seems genuinely happy to see us after so many years, insists on giving us her version of the facts. And so we learn, as the truth works its way through her disconnected narrative, that the more Dragan "freed up" the territories taken by the enemy, the more Jasna's material dreams took shape. After a year of war, she'd hired soldiers from her husband's unit to build a swimming pool on the roof of her immense penthouse with windowed walls. With the signing of the Dayton Accords, which marked the end of the hostilities, Dragan was perhaps a hero and a prosperous man, but five years of war had seriously compromised his health, which his wife had thought to be unassailable. Dayton appeared to Dragan as an angel of salvation. And then, two years after the fighting ended, he had a heart attack that killed him ten days later. Shocked and disheartened by the sudden weakness of her larger-than-life servitor, Jasna at first refused to visit the hospital, but her children finally convinced her to be there for his end. "You can't leave me alone now," she kept repeating. "How am I going to finish the house by the sea? And the hotel we were going to buy in Istria?"

At the funeral, stiff as a rod, she maintained, at first, a pose as dry-eyed and emotionless as Margaret Thatcher. But when she saw, through the dark glasses hiding half her face, that the whole city had come out to pay homage to her giant, she at last collapsed onto his coffin. "Forgive me, my love. It's all my fault! What good are all my possessions if I don't have you by me?" Then, feeling all eyes fixed upon her, she quickly righted herself. "You all take yourselves for saints? Only yesterday, you were murderers! Be careful, I have the proofs, black on white, of all your crimes!"

Dragan had survived the war, but his wife's consuming ambition had killed him bit by bit. So as to distance himself from her, he'd gone to ground in the wooden cabin he built with his own hands at the foot of Mount Velež, to write his memoirs. When he died, Jasna promptly took possession of the writings her husband had hoped to publish one day. She had in her hands the undisclosed narrative, by a direct witness, of the bloody events of the Balkan war. Her husband's memoirs soon proved themselves to be her best capital. Whenever she had a whim, whether for a sailboat or an apartment in Venice, for example, Jasna demanded impressive sums in exchange for a few manuscript pages, which she offered to the local tabloids run by war criminals, but also to the justice system and international institutions for human rights. In the end, she had done well to heed her husband and remain in Mostar. Who knows what would have happened had Gaddafi chosen her, rather than Safia? All's well that ends well, she tells herself every night, sipping a martini and leafing through design magazines by the side of her swimming pool, cut off from the world and herself, with her sole distraction friends from another life who, like us, return from afar and seek to understand what has happened to the country since their departure.

Between two visits to Jasna, who showers us with her stories, we try to resume the normal course of our lives. You spend your days looking for an apartment where we will feel at home. Mama tries to enroll us in school and to find herself a job, but everything is difficult, laborious. We see that Mostar has changed, that the people we knew are no longer there, and that a return to normality is an illusion. As all privileges are reserved for those who stayed and fought in the war, we feel like intruders in our own city. You become increasingly discouraged, not because of the demands of everyday life, but because you are aware of navigating an unhealthy environment where the war has come to an end on paper only. The other war, that of mentalities and resentments, rages on, since Mostar remains divided by an invisible frontier fully recognized by the populace on both banks of the river. Football matches pitting the two teams, Croatian and Bosnian, against each other, are particularly violent, and you fear for the safety of your children, especially when drunkards start playing with snipers' guns and bombs to add a little atmosphere. The more your friends tell you about the details of the war, the more you sink into an abyss where only alcohol gives you some respite. You feel guilty both for not having been present to fight by the side of your own people, and for having returned your children to a country where scores are far from being settled. Mama seems a bit more discouraged every day. She spends her time at the window of our new apartment. She misses Switzerland and its social peace, despite her hard work as a chambermaid. As for me, repelled by your inability to take things in hand, I decide to act. I get back in touch with the Canadian Red Cross in Geneva, which

had offered us the possibility of emigrating to Canada. Before
deciding to return to Bosnia, we'd made an application. Our
request was accepted, and if we want, we can still take advantage of it. The single condition is that we leave from Geneva,
finalizing the arrangements in Switzerland. I await the first
opportunity to inform you of my decision. At the table, I
announce that I'm leaving alone for America and will get
you out of your bind afterwards. You drop your fork, while
Mama and little brother burst into tears. After a long silence,
you look me straight in the eye and declare in all solemnity
that the family will not separate: we'll leave together for the
New World. A month later, we're back in Geneva, in transit
this time, waiting for the family visa that will open Canada's
doors for us. Before leaving Mostar forever, you had turned
your head, just barely, to murmur these few words: "I only
returned the better to leave again."

Just before leaving Switzerland, my kid brother and I
go off on the sly to visit Paris. Two streets from our hotel, a
cultural association is paying homage to Andrei Tarkovski.
I enter the theatre by chance. The shock of this encounter
with the Russian filmmaker is absolute. I find something of
you in each of his shots, and in each of his tragically Slavic
characters I think I recognize one of your many faces. At that
moment I'm not entirely aware of the impact that *Nostalghia*
will have on me, but I already know that the story of the character in this film is in part your own. The poet Gorchakov,
accompanied by his sublime translator, Eugenia, crosses Italy
on the trail of a compatriot, a composer who trod the same
ground two centuries earlier. Gorchakov stops in an ancient
village that once sheltered the composer when he was in
search of inspiration. It was in this pagan village that the poet
learned about the mad Domenico. He had imprisoned his
family for seven years to save them from the evil rampant in
the world. Gorchakov, overwhelmed by his own nostalgia for
his land and his family, and obsessed by the ambivalence of

his feelings for the young Italian translator, hears everywhere the cries of the mad Domenico, who over the course of the film becomes his alter ego. Domenico embodies, from the moment of his appearance, the dark side of the central character: the lure of the abyss. The last scene of *Nostalghia* sums up Tarkovski's vision of the world: the madman immolates himself on the public square, refusing to belong to a humanity that has lost its sense of brotherhood and simplicity.

Suddenly, I understand that the nostalgia eating away at your insides, and your desire to make heard the voices of the past in order to save the present, condemn you to walk the fine line that separates you from madness. The Russian poet, exiled in Italy, lost like you in his imaginary lands, sees *through* Domenico's madness to his refusal of a materialist, chauvinist, ideological, and religious world. It is madness that gains us access to a more liberating world. Towards the end of the film, panic-stricken on the public square, Domenico invites the masses, whom he calls "soft brains," statuettes stock-still in their solitude, to return to the essentials of life, far from hatred and vain quests. I watch the film's last scene, my mouth agape, not knowing if you remind me more of the nostalgic poet or of the madman speaking to all humankind. How not to think of you who, every time the outside world harms your little tribe, tries to save it while flying off towards other horizons? How not to see Domenico in you when you try to make your compatriots understand that they are wrong to cling to their murderous identities, and when you try to make them understand that life is elsewhere, in beauty, in art, in sunlit cities. Since this providential encounter with Tarkovski, I've seen *Nostalghia* many times, especially after stumbling on the filmmaker's photograph in a film magazine: he resembles you more than your twin brother. He died, like you, of lung cancer, on a 29th of December, the day after your birthday.

On the last night of our Paris adventure, exhausted from walking all day, we watch French television in our hotel room.

Bored by the news about starlets, I turn off the TV set and turn on the radio. I come to a station that broadcasts music from around the world. Little brother is stretched out on the bed, playing Nintendo. Between two songs, a journalist starts talking about an event that has taken place in front of the United Nations building in Geneva. Swiss special forces have had to bring down a deranged individual who climbed onto a sculpture in the Place des Nations: "Today, at around one o'clock, a Bosnian refugee laid siege to artist Daniel Berset's monumental sculpture. The refugee was removed and placed in detention. The man demanded an end to nationalism and a return to the brotherhood promoted by Tito. He threatened to jump from the wooden sculpture, a giant chair with a torn leg, which represents the struggle for peace and the fight against anti-personnel mines."

Before moving on to athletic exploits at Wimbledon, the station transmits the refugee's voice, in simultaneous translation: "You, workers of the United Nations, seated comfortably in your chairs! Read the definition of the word 'refugee': a person who has had to flee the place where he lives in order to escape from danger! But tell me, where will we flee when the earth is no longer able to bear our egotism, our delusions of grandeur, and the profit-sickness that eats away at true human values? Man is a spiritual being who needs visionaries and humanism! You, with your theories and empty talk, do something concrete: give me back my country! Give me back my life, my bridge, my city! Give me back all my friends!"

On our return from Paris, I know that the time has come for us to leave Switzerland and try our luck elsewhere, far from Europe and its leaden memories. The day we leave for America, Mama and the kid brother are both in tears while you and I sing the New World's praises. You're as excited as a child by this new departure. I now know your routine by heart, the same one that's repeated in every country where you set foot: excitation, disenchantment, free-fall. As we fly

over the Canadian landscape and you look down, the joy in
your voice diminishes. You are silent before these immense,
empty spaces, with here and there a few habitable spots, lost
among the lakes and rivers as wide as the European seas
and waterways. You sense populations thrown together in
patches randomly scattered, with no centre, no link between
one city and another. All that, seen from on high, disappoints
and frightens you. "It's not what I thought. But, well, we'll
just prolong our winter vacation and go back home in the
spring!" A tragic premonition raises a lump in my throat. I
feel that America for you will be a departure with no return,
and that you'll never see Europe again. In this metal machine
advancing between two continents, between before and after,
I play Barbara's music at full volume in my earphones, to
silence my suspicions:

> *When those who go, who part and go,*
> *When the last day has dawned*
> *In the pale yellow light,*
> *When those who go, who part and go,*
> *For always and forever*
> *Deep beneath the earth*

As soon as we set down on Canadian soil, we must once
more spend an indeterminate amount of time in a refugee
centre while our papers are put in order. We're so used to
these transitory places that they have almost become a normal way of living in the world. No need to explain the rules,
we know them by heart. But one thing strikes us immediately
in the middle of Ottawa: those who hold power and make
the rules are immigrants. There is no superior attitude on
the part of the "locals" towards the "foreigners," as in Europe.
Our social worker is Guatemalan, the director of the centre
is Lebanese, and the manager of the canteen is an Egyptian
Copt. Our window gives onto King Edward Street and the

Department of Foreign Affairs. Mama dreams of seeing me work in that kind of building one day. When, a few years later, I find myself teaching French in the building in question to a deputy minister whose window looks out on our first Canadian residence, I think to myself that, despite all one might say about America, it's still a continent of immigrants where anything is possible. This continent, for me, is the beginning of my island, your premonition. At the age of nineteen I cannot yet understand what frightens you so. My youthful naivety permits me to believe that all you have to do is make an effort to assimilate, to learn the language, to take an interest in other people, and it's a done deal. But you turn my words back on me when you reply:

"For a deal to be done, you have to be young and in revolt against a place that's standing in the way of your getting ahead. Only then can you gather the strength to turn your back on it. You found Switzerland suffocating, isn't that why you wanted to leave for America?"

"Yes . . ."

"When Yahweh asked Abraham to leave Ur, his native city, he obeyed because the order came from God. Me, it's men who made me leave. And orders from men are worthless. When he's forced to do something by his fellows, a man is like a child who balks: he does things resentfully or not at all."

As I got older, I reached a better understanding of your refusal to go along with the American Dream by becoming a perfect immigrant. Almost from the start, the immensity, the individualism, the over-consumption, the capitalism, the invented, tailor-made identities, the ugliness of young cities with no history, weighed on you. As for me, there was nothing more that I could do for you.

CEDAR HILL
BERRY FARM

I STILL DON'T KNOW how to make a distinction between homesickness and one's nostalgia for childhood. To want to recover the country that inhabits our memories and dreams, is this not to yearn for the lightheartedness and verve of our early years? When you are forced to flee the land of your birth, one question nags at you constantly: "And if there had been no war?" Would our nostalgia then have been any different from that of Proust? In Canada, each of us does his or her best to stay afloat. You spend your days painting images from the past, and inventing colours for the future. The present tense is but a way station for you, a necessary evil, while we, we try to persuade ourselves that on this continent where everything is possible, happiness is there to be grasped; we just have to *show our determination* to turn the page and move on. But you know that you never move on when the past is what's most important to you. And yet, sometimes, passing through a valley, in the shade of a mulberry tree, or, at the foot of a hill that calls out to our memories, we sometimes want to stop and believe, for a season, that we have again found a piece of our lost paradise, and that it is still possible to start over.

The immense agricultural property of Cedar Hill in the Ottawa Valley, between Pakenham and Almonte, clings jealously to its past. In this peaceful spot on the banks of the Mississippi River (not the legendary one), Canadians defended their borders against the Americans during the nineteenth century. Almonte was in fact named after a Mexican general who had also resisted American expansionism. But before the birth of its founding myth—forged, as usual, by war—the little town had seen the light thanks to a Scottish adventurer called David Shepherd. He'd left the old country in 1810 to set up the region's first watermill, lending the village its first name: Mississippi Mills. Almonte was known for its textile factories before the industry went into decline in the 1980s. Since then, it's been a tourist spot dotted with waterfalls and little museums.

In his native Ireland, William Forsyth had perhaps heard talk of the good fortune a certain Scot had enjoyed in America. Feeling stifled by the narrowness of mind and many wars rampant in Europe, he decided he, too, would try his luck. He left Ireland to settle in 1820 on a vast farm in the Ottawa Valley. At the time, the British government was almost giving land away in order to populate the vast Canadian landscape. The family that owns the farm now is a direct descendant of this sturdy man who came to America to breathe new life into the destiny of his clan. Over the centuries, Forsyth's farm became a property of several hundred acres where strawberries, raspberries, blueberries, corn, and Christmas trees were grown. Cedar Hill Berry Farm, on Sundays after Mass, serves as a meeting place where a whole community comes from afar to pick berries or cut down fir trees, depending on the season. The farm also attracts local youth, who work there to earn pocket money. Far from the tumult of civilization, these blonde, red-cheeked adolescents lead a simple, healthy life. To talk to them for a moment is to be reminded of childhood's pantheism, when nature, heaven, and man are one, and when, with one's hair in the wind and a pure heart, there is no distinction to be made between a zest for life and the stirring of a transcendence that some call God. The farm, surrounded by fir trees, with its wooden houses and their porches where wide sofas rock back and forth, evokes for me the magical mysteries of *Little House on the Prairie*, which set all of Eastern Europe to dreaming.

The summer we arrive in Canada you resent having to live again on social assistance, but one has to make do before finding a real trade. In any case, the sums we receive from the Canadian government are not enough to feed us. It's after seeing a small ad in a newspaper that I call the Cedar Hill farm. That summer, the land has proved fertile, and the owner is looking desperately for strawberry pickers. All three of us are hired on the spot. As of the next day, we begin to write the most beautiful pages of our life in Canada. You're the first to rise, at five o'clock in the morning. You make sandwiches for everybody, you grind and put the *bosanska kahva*, the Turkish coffee, on to boil, you spread butter and honey on toast before finally coming to gently wake us up. No one, since the beginning of the war, has seen you so enthusiastic. And yet the work we're to do is for the most part thankless. But the mirages that hover over the immense Ontario plains, the deep, low sky, like that in a painting that conceals its mystery, the many streams that point to the tumultuous waterways whose tributaries they are, the sun-gorged fruit sold by the roadside, the solitary houses along peaceful golden paths, all that, you say, reminds you of Adriatic mornings, before the devastation. Every time you spot the farm I glimpse in your eye the same joy that gripped you when you rediscovered the sea in your country. In this remote place, lost in Canadian forests, did your own, personal Atlantis emerge from the depths of your unconscious? Was it your artist's imagination that overflowed, or simply the morning dew that touched, for the first time in so many years, your heart bruised by the war?

On the farm, before sunrise, an acid mist creeps between bushes weighed down by small red berries. Silence reigns. We hear nothing but the echo of the loons' cries on the nearby lakes, and the rubbing of straw on the backsides of the pickers, who have had to relearn how to crawl, like babies. Otherwise, there prevails a silence from beyond the grave, which the flies will come to disturb with their frenetic dance shortly before noon, when the picking stops. On the veranda, you smoke while fixing your eyes on a spot directly in front of you, and you tell the farmer, every time he comes by to see you, that his farm is a place of "therapy" for you. He understands, beyond the gulf that separates your two languages, that you are a tormented soul for whom happiness is but a distant memory. He tries to console you by talking about your "magnificent" children, and about their future in Canada. You continue to view the world like an autistic child who wonders what he's doing there. With the money earned from the day's harvest, and immediately pocketed, we leave, happy, to sip coffee in Almonte.

You like this place more than any other because the waterfalls, the mulberry trees, and the benches, carved into by lovers, make you think of Buna, the vacation spot thirty or so kilometres from Mostar, where you loved to spend time after work. Above all, Almonte has the quiet charm of places that have a centre, and a history whose continuity is assured by a number of families. Even if the farm isn't open on the Lord's day, you insist on driving to Almonte on Sundays to see the community exiting the church, shaking hands, talking of all or nothing. You love to watch the old people eating their sunny-side-up eggs, their baked beans, and their toast and peanut butter in the little restaurant full of Elvis Presley photos. Everything makes you think of your homeland, even if you observe this society without understanding English. A painter is always, you tell me, outside language. Despite your flights of oratory you've never really been a man of words, but I try all the same to persuade you that, in order to feel at ease in another culture, you must master the other's language.

"You can be happy in another language. I'm more likely going to die in my Slavic *baraka*, where you speak the language of the deaf." The eternal prophet, you still talk in parables, and every one of your sentences takes my breath away. What are you trying to say, in the end? Your native language, Serbo-Croatian, is a Slavic language riddled with words from Latin, Turkish, Persian, Greek, German, Hungarian—I could go on. The "language of the deaf" is the language of painters? Or are you talking about the dialogue of the deaf in which the Balkans have been immersed since the beginning?

Even after the picking season is over, you return to Almonte on Sundays and Mondays to savour the tranquillity of a day of rest, and the energy of a week's beginning. To be a perfect intruder into another culture, you say, you just have to speak the language of feeling. Like a thief, on the tips of your toes, with your paintbrush and a few pencils, you steal away, making off with a few scraps of the Almonte dwellers' lives. During this time I'm devouring novels under the mulberry tree near the mill. You come back with a notebook full of sketches, and you explain to me the nuances with which you intend to paint these people on the margins of history. No need to contend with the imperfection of words. One day, seeing that I'm immersed in my book, you start asking me questions. I'm reading *The Bookseller of Kabul*, by Åsne Seierstad. A Norwegian journalist posted to Kabul, she was taken in during the war by an Afghan family. I explain that her book fascinates me because she was able to witness and describe intimate scenes, to familiarize herself with the customs and rules and regulations of the country, to faithfully render her characters' interior monologues. Thanks to her, we, the outsiders, know the inner logic of Afghan culture a bit better. Incredulous, you jerk your head as if to dismiss everything I've been saying.

"This book is fiction, or a document?"

"I think it's a well-documented novel."

"Then it's a fiction."

"No, she really lived with a family."

"Ah yes? And what are those intimate scenes she was able to witness? She saw the patriarch making love with his wife? So she knows about Afghan sexuality?"

I don't know what to reply. My imagination, without being aware of it, has passed over those moments where the author could not be present. And so the book is fiction. You laugh and then you warn me: I have to take care not to be contaminated by the virus of Western omniscience. "They know everything. They see everything. They decide every-thing," you tell me, before proceeding with the interrogation.

"And tell me, in what language are you reading this book?"

"In French. It's translated from the Norwegian."

"And she? What language did she speak with the Afghans? Norwegian?"

"No, she had translators into English."

You burst out laughing.

"She knew neither Pashto nor Urdu. She trusted people who told her about the reality of this family in English, so as to then write in Norwegian for you to read her in a French translation. From Pashto to English, from English to Norwe-gian, from Norwegian to French: a fount of falsehoods."

"But if I follow your reasoning, we have no real access to any literature other than that whose original language we've mastered!"

"It's more complicated than that, daughter! I assume, with-out having read her book, that this Norwegian—who is cer-tainly blonde, tall, and feminist—has simplified many things, most likely setting her sights on Afghan men's machismo?"

"Yes."

"I'm tired of those Westerners who claim to understand the worlds of others! The Bernard-Henri Lévys and their gang, who go to Sarajevo to pound their chests in solidarity with Bosnian civilians, whereas in reality everything is always focused on themselves. She's understood nothing, your Norwegian, of Afghan culture, and if I were this Kabul bookseller, this man who had the kindness and naiveté to welcome her into his private space, I'd sue her!"

A bomb is going to explode in the centre of my chest. I'm outraged at this knack you have of performing vivisections on writers without even opening their books. I muck around in the mire of words while you, you present a world that is truer and more transparent. On your sketches of Almonte faces, not a hint of judgment.

"Your journalist would have had to know how to describe the tenderness of the couple, which she obviously never saw. To talk well about love, you have to have loved enough yourself . . . But that's the whole story of men who, badly loved, perpetuate this lack of love, this endless chain of suffering from generation to generation . . ."

Later, reading a more subtle writer, I remembered this conversation, and I understood what you were really seeking in Almonte. In *The Fragile Lights of Earth*, Gabrielle Roy embeds herself in the daily life of a Mennonite family living apart from the world on the endless Manitoba plains. For these people, the very existence of the outside world has been taboo ever since the first family arrived from Pennsylvania and began to write on the still-virgin page of their life in Canada. Closed off in the impeccable logic of daily ancestral rituals apportioned according to sex and age before they even come into the world, every member of the clan knows his or her place. Only a blind and assiduous repetition can preserve the memory and ensure the survival of the group. The Old Order Mennonites live as on the first day of their founding myth, remote from industrialization and modern life. They work the land, follow the path of the sun to measure time, eat their own produce, and love God passionately. To break this perfect circle is to introduce death into the heart of the group. Spending time with the Mennonites, the writer experiences, beyond the sadness an outsider may feel in contact with the circle's tenuous nature, the comforting pleasure to be found in such continuity.

Thanks to Gabrielle Roy's writings, I suddenly understand your disarray, faced with the New World. You were driven away from your home, your lineage's history has a curse on it, like that of the Balkans in general, but, unlike your elders, you have the opportunity to start with a clean slate, like William Forsyth when he set down his bags in the Ottawa Valley, and like the first Mennonites arriving in Winnipeg. Can one not reinvent true freedom? I try to convince you of it to allay your suffering, I try to make you see that it's all a matter of perspective, and that, instead of lamenting your fate, you can begin a "new life," in deference to your own laws. With all of Slavic tragedy before your eyes, and all your Eastern fatalism on your lips, you put me in my place: "The New World's naiveté has already got under your skin. You believe stupidly in the American Dream, and in the power of a solitary man. But I'm weak and cowardly, like Ulysses, who wants nothing to do with the marvels he encounters along his way. Like him, I just want to find my native land again!"

After this conversation, I began to see the shadow of death hovering over your head. I understood then that you were doomed to live in an imaginary world. You yearned to regain a country that no longer existed, and the invisible cities that you glimpsed as mirages in the boundless Canadian landscape were perhaps nothing more than apparitions out of another world, which you would soon be joining. Waiting to regain your vanished Ithaca, nostalgic, and envious of a normal life that wanted nothing of you, you returned regularly underneath the Almonte mulberry tree near the old mill, to observe in silence a community outside of time, whose beige, uneventful pages were unstained by history's black ink. May this monotony endure, and may history's grandeur take no notice of you, ever. That is all you wished for the inhabitants of the Ottawa Valley. But also for all other earthlings.

CUBA,
PARADISE LOST

THE FIRST THING you notice in Montreal, even before the panhandlers and the astonishing mildness of the Indian Summer, are the posters advertising Cuba. You are astonished to learn that Castro's island is your new compatriots' favourite tourist destination: over a million Canadians visit every year. You feel from the very start an urgency to go there, because the island evokes, in your mind as in mine, a lost paradise. But this project is put off time and again. I've already been several times—I even wrote my first book there—and I cherish the hope that there you will rediscover, for the first time since the war, the anomaly of a society where the capitalism you abhor has not yet done its worst.

I recounted in my book that I found in Havana's streets the same uniform for little pioneers that I wore in Tito's Yugoslavia, the omnipresence of the State, the "Communist taste" of the local ice cream, the people who live their lives with open doors, the parties and meals improvised at street corners, the musicians styled like Roma, the women with false nails who wear nylon stockings despite the punishing heat, but also the existential question that gnaws away at all the inhabitants: stay or leave? But you cannot read me in the language I've chosen for my writing. I don't know what words to use to explain to you my love at first sight for the Cuban sea, which makes me so much think of the Adriatic, source of all our happy memories, but also of your unhappiness since the day when, upon its back, chased off by the war, we distanced ourselves forever from our country. I don't know how to explain to you that the Cubans also have a problematic relationship with the sea: for those who have decided to stay, the ocean that surrounds their island is an immense source of happiness and dreams. For the others, the *balseros* who have decided to leave, it's a cruel threat: many clandestine rafts sink with all hands on board during their voyage to the promised land of Florida. Nor do I know how to tell you that, thanks to you and all you've taught me, I've found in Cuba not only a balm for the melancholy caused by our traumatic uprooting, but a land, perhaps the only one in the world, where I feel truly at peace.

Seeing you in such a bad state and so disappointed in the American continent, I try to persuade you to follow me, telling you that Cuba could very well be the island you've so often described to me, the one that would show you it's still possible to have ideals. But you don't want to hear about it. Like all depressives you derive satisfaction from your unhappiness, and your turning in circles has become almost a way of being. And the idea of taking another plane deeply disturbs you. I see that the only thing that might finally persuade you to make the trip is the possibility of seeing your friend Padre Nicolò once more. When Fra Ivan came to find you and Mama to get you out of the war, he was accompanied by this young philanthropic priest who, having inherited a family fortune, decided to help the poor and excluded of this world. Leaving the camp, you soon became fast friends, as he was passionate about painting and sculpture. After our departure for Switzerland, and Padre Nicolò's posting to Africa, he never lost contact with our family. Just before leaving for Canada, we received a letter in which he informed us of another mission, to Cuba. For you, it was one more sign that you must absolutely go there . . . one day.

It took Hurricane Katrina in New Orleans for you to at last make up your mind. Furious at this humanitarian catastrophe and its shameful mismanagement, you curse the Americans, who can finance their war in Iraq, but can't help the poor people in Louisiana going through hell right before their eyes, as in a reality TV show. "Cuba is subject to hurricanes every year, and have you ever heard of such a catastrophe down there? Never! And you know why? Because the State doesn't care about the economy when a hurricane comes through, Fidel mobilizes everything! In America, if the government took such a decision, do you know how many millionaires would be sounding the alarm? All of them, to the very last one! Because in the meanwhile, they wouldn't be making any profit!"

Two days after Katrina passes, you announce that you intend to come with me on my next visit to the island, and that you hope to experience a hurricane along with the islanders, to admire "this little country under embargo, which has so much to teach the entire world." I schedule my next stay for the extreme east of the island, where I want to begin writing my new book. I buy you an airplane ticket, and you jump up and down like a child whose most cherished dream has just come true. You call your friend Slobodan, in Switzerland, and you shout into the telephone: "Slobo! I'm going to see Castro!" Slobodan, like all the people your age who believed firmly in the solidarity and strength of the Yugoslav people, has always admired Cuba. This distant and mythic satellite of the socialist world has fed the dreams of entire generations.

We get off the plane in Baracoa, and the first thing that strikes you are the smiles of the customs inspectors when you pull out your Bosnian passport. Here, for the first time since you left your country, you're greeted with open arms because you're a communist! You're delighted when you see the lengthy questioning to which the English tourists must submit, despite passports that everywhere command respect. "For once, we're welcome somewhere." What you find beautiful in the New World is that it has not yet been tainted to its very core by an obsession with identities. Cubans know very little about our absurd ethnic wars. For them, we're still Yugoslav comrades. You're especially impressed by the lack of advertising, omnipresent in the airports of "democratic" countries. A muscular old man with drinker's breath offers us a rustic means of transport: the *bicitaxi*. He's caught your eye, and you decide that it's with him that we'll make our way into the city. I install myself as comfortably as I can on the boiling hot leather seat, one hand on our little suitcase, the other on the bottle of iced water I hold between my thighs to refresh myself. Against all expectations, you ask to pedal in his place, to make his job easier. Stunned by the gesture, he turns to me every three seconds to tell me that there's no need to help him, that no one ever pedals for him. I carefully monitor your reaction, and I see that you're already mad about Cuba. Everything delights you, especially the dusty children brimming over with joy who are playing outside to the point of exhaustion.

When we arrive at the centre of Baracoa, not far from the statue of Christopher Columbus, you marvel at the sea air. The children who live in the houses giving onto the ocean are playing at *trombo*, the spinning top on a rope that's the island's most popular game, and a pastime for most adults as well. It's morning. Baracoa is just coming to life. The Russian truck that transports workers is stopping at strategic places along the Malecón, which rims the shore. You don't understand Spanish, but you know that the short, quick phrases the men are addressing to the women, in the style of "Beauty, you eat too much meat!" have nothing nasty about them. The old Russian and American cars pass carts and *bicitaxis* like ours, which tacks like a drunken boat around the many pot-holes. A thick fog is rising like a ghost come out of the sea to coax faces back into sleep. The aroma of freshly ground coffee mingles with the wafts of iodine that help the city to waken. You observe, wide-eyed, the schoolchildren coming out of their houses, and you see, as I'd told you, that they are indeed wearing the same young pioneer uniforms as did little Yugoslavs. The streets, finally, are buzzing with life, and I see, for the first time in so many years, tears of joy in your eyes, which are so often clouded.

We set our suitcases down in our room at the La Rusa Hotel, where I usually stay. You like the place, which is my favourite spot in Baracoa. And you're moved when I tell you that Che slept in this very room. Since the beginning of the revolution, the hotel's owner, of White Russian background, supported the Castrists against Batista. As we talk, the wind strikes the shutters, and then, insistent, swings them open suddenly to reveal the sea. Dazzled, you murmur: "You'd think it was the Adriatic." You understand why I love this city, the first one founded by the Spanish in Cuba. Unlike Havana, Baracoa is not a tourist destination. Here, time has stopped since the era of the conquistadors. Silence descends on our room. We listen to the sound of the waves, and of the day that's beginning. You make a remark that has me doubting your lack of interest in literature. "Something in this little town reminds me of *One Hundred Years of Solitude.*" It's true that you have only to stroll through the streets of this city, remote from the world, to see the resemblance to Gar-cía Márquez's descriptions. The ghost of magic realism floats over Baracoa.

The Colombian writer is even said to have claimed it was Baracoa that inspired his most famous novel. Charac-ters from another world hide behind their straw hats, houses rise up among the leaves of giant palms and banana trees, coachmen with sunburnt faces drive their carriages, the most popular means of transport, the relentless humidity penetrates pores and minds, alcohol and music flow freely, phantoms rub shoulders with the living, and abundant rains offer a sense of renewal, even if nothing erases the communist slogans. "In what language did you read García Márquez?" You don't answer. Instead, you light a cigar that you'll smoke avidly without taking your eyes off the sea.

We go out into the street, as you're eager to take possession of the city. All Baracoa's streets lead to the Malecón, the wide promenade that follows the shoreline, which, with its steep rocks, really does recall the Adriatic coast. Seeing an old man tossing garbage into the sea, I stop to ask him why he's contaminating the environment this way. His name is Dalí. He's black, and has several gold teeth. He avoids answering my question by instead telling me he's the only jazz singer in Baracoa. But when I persist, he explains: "I earn 400 pesos a month. What am I to do, miss? Eat for 200 pesos and spend the other 200 to have my garbage picked up?"

You've guessed the tenor of our conversation, and you chide me: "Stop thinking like those damn capitalists! The Americans and the Europeans care about the environment, it's their new crusade, but they're still consuming like madmen and sending airplanes filled with their garbage, now, all the way to China. Stop thinking like those hypocrites and leave the poor devil in peace. He's not the problem. It's the damn embargo on his island that's lasted for fifty years."

We continue on our way, and you ask me questions about "*la Rusa*," the late owner of our hotel. I've rarely in my life had the opportunity to teach you anything, and I'm delighted to talk to you about this woman whose life and death have deeply inspired me.

"The Cubans adore her, and she's inspired many writers, including Alejo Carpentier. In *The Rites of Spring*, *la Rusa* is the main character. Magdalenka Rovenskaya—that's her real name—is described there as a mysterious being with one foot in the land of dreams, and the other in life."

"Like me!"

"Her father was a Tsarist soldier killed during the October revolution, and she had to flee Russia at the age of thirteen, with her mother. She took refuge in Turkey, where she ended up marrying Albert Menasse, a Russian diplomat. The couple arrived in Baracoa at the beginning of the 1930s to take over the Menasse family's prosperous business. They rapidly became the owners of many businesses and plantations, but the city of Baracoa had by this time cast such a spell over Magdalena that she decided to stay there forever."

You're listening intently, fascinated by this character, whose portrait you say you want to draw. You light one cigarette after another as we wander through the streets of Baracoa, and I continue the story of *la Rusa*.

"She assumed Cuban nationality in 1944, and never left the island, she who had known international fame. Her magnificent voice had led her to perform at the Paris Opera, at La Scala in Milan, and on many other stages, but success never went to her head, and 'Mimi' was deeply moved by the poverty of the Cuban people under the corrupt and tyrannical rule of the Batista regime."

"She had good reason to be outraged! Without Fidel and his comrades, this would be another Las Vegas, a thousand-footed monster with no head and no tail!"

"And so, even though the Bolsheviks had assassinated all her family, Magdalena embraced the revolution, to which she offered almost all her fortune, putting the largest part of her material wealth at the disposal of the rebels."

"Including the hotel?"

"At that time there was no hotel. It was her principal residence, and there she entertained all the great figures of the Cuban revolution, including Fidel and Raúl Castro, Celia Sánchez, Vilma Espín, Che Guevara, and Aleida March. When nationalization deprived the former masters of their privileges and private property, Fidel, because of *la Rusa*'s unconditional support for the revolution, decided not to dislodge her while she was alive. She would enjoy her house to the end. The day after her death, the building became the property of the government."

You're fascinated by the story of this woman, you want to know everything about her, and above all you want to meet her adopted son, the painter René Format. I take you to see his house, which has been transformed into a museum. René is eighty-eight years old. With one eye on his paintings, the other on the house where he has spent the greatest part of his life, the Hotel La Rusa, he guards the memory of the mysterious Russian woman who landed on the shores of Baracoa. Like most Cubans occupying a "decent" house capable of receiving tourists, René has transformed his dwelling into a *casa particular.* His wife, Lisette, thirty years his junior, takes care of the household, while René spends his days in his little studio.

The old man invites us, with a wave, to sit and listen to the passionate story of his adoptive mother. René asks no questions about our relationship. He probably thinks we're a couple whose age difference in no way shocks him. His museum's dusty display cases are full of jewels, shoes, clothes, and *la Rusa*'s personal possessions, like this wallet with an unpublished picture of the young Fidel. Other photographs and portraits tell the story of her life as a diva. There are pieces of Russian embroidery and the cloth dolls she made for poor children, but also more incongruous articles, like nylon stockings and lace brassieres. René worships his adoptive mother, and the intricate and almost obsessive quality of his paintings points to a somewhat fetishist personality. However, this fervent revolutionary speaks "in the Cuban style," with its macho flavour. He'll let no one speak badly of Fidel. During his story, you touch each of *la Rusa*'s objects.

You ask the old man if he'd agree to sell you one of her corsets. As our host begins to recoil, you explain: "Women's corsets have always fascinated me. They are like a cage for their hearts, which would like to fly away." In violation of his own principles, René in the end agrees to surrender a pale pink corset that smells of dust and rosewater.

We go back to the hotel to drop off *la Rusa's* corset, which you carefully wash and iron. It's only much later that I come to understand what you wanted to use it for. Meanwhile, you are so fascinated by Cuba that you call Mama to ask her to postpone our return date. I have to interview potential characters for future novels and documentaries, and I'd not anticipated that you'd be with me during my long stay. Truth be told, I'm a bit tired of translating Cuba for you. But you insist, and promise you won't ask me for anything more: "In any case, I can feel this country beyond words." Except that in reality, it's another story: you have to go through me, for example, to call Padre Nicolò, and inform him of our arrival. The man himself, learning the news, lets out a cry of joy before asking us to come straight over to see him in his small parish. When he spots us, he runs up and embraces us so enthusiastically that I'm afraid he'll break your small bones. You're just as happy to be reunited with the man who saved our lives. You start at once to talk to him about the war. Nicolò, knowing full well what we've been through, politely evades the subject so as not to reopen old wounds.

Discreetly, he turns the conversation toward our current preoccupations.

Nicolò begins by asking us questions about Fra Ivan, his close friend, who was of so much help to us. Then he launches into his explanations for the pathetic state of Baracoa. He tells us that the town was recently devastated by the *mare de leva*. Part of the lower town lost walls and roofs, and its three-century-old cathedral, the town's pride and joy, has lost its bell tower. The presbytery, right next to the cathedral,

is a blue-and-yellow jewel. As the priest tells us about life in
Baracoa, people come in and go out, sometimes interrupting
the conversation. We can tell right away that Nicolò is much
loved by his parishioners. Born in Bolzano, in the Italian
Tyrol, he knew very early on that he wanted to be a priest and
to spend his life serving others. He has long hair, a poet's little
beard, and wears wide white robes that remind me of Saudi
princes. He jogs every day, and like every good Italian would
give his life for his football team. He also loves the arts and
literature, and dreams of one day having the time to write his
memoirs. But he sees himself as still too young for such an
enterprise, even if he would have much to tell.

In another life, when he was still in Italy, just before arriving in Yugoslavia during the conflict, he dealt with the unfortunate Roma, who, in a so-called civilized Europe, no one
treated as true human beings. It is they, Nicolò tells us, who
taught him the value of living in the present. Besides, that is
all he preaches: to live for the present moment as if it were the
last. Does that mean that life after death, the paradise promised by the Catholic Church, is the least of his concerns? In
your more than adequate Italian, you begin to ask him existential questions. And then, as if I were not there, but with
my help, you embark on a dialogue that I've never been able
to forget:

"Life after death? My friend, to tell the truth, I hardly ever
think about it. Why bother? I've so many things to do here
below. I leave this task to the priests in the Vatican. I have
other things to do."

"You Italians, you've always loved life and beautiful things.
You talk about the Roma, but this philosophy of the present
moment, the Cubans have it too, no?"

"You're right. When I arrived here, I truly came to understand what that means, to live in the present. Because here,
that's all that counts: to eat, to drink, to dance, today. Tomorrow, we'll see. And above all, we don't care!"

"But isn't it a bit natural to think that way in a city so often subject to hurricanes? The last one, with this *bar de leva* you were talking about earlier, swept everything away in its wake, houses, animals, and men. Just one wave that swallowed up everything in its path. . . That would have done us a lot of good, we Yugos, to have a dangerous climate that could take our minds off our stupid differences."

"Yes and no. The Cubans are like that wherever they are, even where there are no hurricanes. All they know to do in life is dance and complain. And they complain about everything: the country's political situation, the heat, the embargo, the tourists, the bland coffee, racial discrimination, filthy streets, antisocial behaviour, everything. But they don't know how to organize to make things better. They put everything on the back of Fidel, the revolution, and the embargo that stands in the way of their progress. It's true that Fidel is omnipresent, and that in this country you feel like you're in the land of Orwell: everything you do is being observed. By the way, they already know who you are, and that at this very moment you're talking to me. You'll see, in a few minutes a pretty young woman is going to come over and greet me. She's part of the Seguridad, the political police. But let's get back to our subject. Here, if things don't progress, it's not because of Fidel, it's because of the citizens, each of whom is more spineless than the next. But you can move things along here. I've done it!"

Suddenly, a young tigress, well turned out, comes up to us. She introduces herself, shakes our hands, and kisses Padre Nicolò on the cheek. Then she inquires about our visit, checks us over from head to toe, and asks the priest for our names. To our great surprise, he answers: "Cassandra, *mi amor*, may I present my friend Ferdinand and his wife, Isabel of Castille."

The young woman knows he's teasing her, even if she doesn't seem too familiar with the history of the Spanish Inquisition. She turns on her heels in a flash, and the priest goes on with his story:

"A few years ago, right after the passage of Ike, the terrible cyclone, I didn't wait for Fidel to give me permission to roll up my sleeves. After seeing the sad state of people living near the sea, I divided the sector into four zones. I distributed canned goods, sheets, utensils, sugar, coffee, and caramels, and I let the humanitarian organizations in Italy know about the disaster in Cuba. A short time later a container of humanitarian aid, filled with food and clothes, was sent in my name to the parish address. What I didn't know is that everything, absolutely everything that arrives in Cuba, must pass through the government. At first I gave the government, which assured me that the distribution would be transparent, the benefit of the doubt. But a short time after the container arrived in Baracoa, wandering through stores, I saw that the preserves that had been sent to help the people survive were being sold in convertible pesos. The bureaucrats were selling off the humanitarian aid illegally, and the money was going straight into their pockets. I immediately complained to the Central Committee of the Revolution in Havana. After a one-year battle, my cause was heard: all the bureaucrats responsible for the theft were fired, and the aid meant for the poor reached them at last."

Both of us were mesmerized by the picture he painted of his adoptive country. I could easily detect the disappointment on your face: you were disenchanted because you had to let go of the idea to which you had clung for so long, that communism was the least corrupt of systems. But Nicolò wasn't finished:

"The critical cast of mind does not exist here, and it's understandable, because the old Greek ideas of the agora, of public space, and even of law, have never really put down roots. You must also not forget what is specific to islanders: they are both extremely open and extremely closed. The climate, and the constant sun, predisposes them to laziness. Fellini got the wrong country: Cubans are the true champions of *la dolce vita*. You know, Fidel is without doubt a dictator, but you can't blame him for everything. The poor man, he can try to keep his eye on everything, to see everything, but omniscience is a divine faculty."

"Actions and words like yours must be seen as reactionary and dissident, no? People must think that if you're being heard, it's because you're a foreigner, no?"

Before replying, the priest lowers his head and shuts his eyes. He gives the impression of having made a vow of silence, but it doesn't last.

"Maybe you're right. But let me tell you that the Cubans exasperate me. Hurricane victims grumble that the State has cast them adrift, and that no one but the Church has come to see them. So now they only believe in us. And in Fidel."

"This faith is rather refreshing for a priest, is it not?"

"But it leads nowhere! A hurricane comes to wake them up for a moment, but they quickly go back to being whining zombies who take no concrete initiatives. They lead a lazy life surrounded by beautiful women, that's all. I've nothing against beautiful women, on the contrary. But you can't choose sex over the economy!"

In the midst of Nicolò's lament, a sublime *jinetera*, a Caribbean Cleopatra, interrupts to confirm her presence at mass on Sunday. You have to help him recover his train of thought:

"What do you talk to them about then, these sheep who want only to hear about you and Fidel?"

"I talk to them about the mystery of the Trinity and the Holy Spirit, at least as I interpret it. Have you ever heard about the true secret of the Vatican?"

"They say that there are many . . ."

"The greatest is that the Holy Spirit, overlapping the Father and the Son, is a woman. The Vatican is a male chauvinist institution that dares not admit that the Spirit is the feminine incarnation par excellence. That is why the Marian cult is

omnipresent. Catholicism's true mysteries are always mysteries of the feminine. Besides, Mary Magdalene was made pregnant by Christ, and their offspring was feminine."

"All that the Cubans understood long before the Vatican!"

"Ha! You're right. The cult of the woman in Cuba is the
cult of the Holy Spirit. Jesus was the first communist, and
Fidel is his apostle."

While Padre Nicolò is amusing himself reinventing Catholic doctrine, World Cup football is going strong. Suddenly
he gets up, and calls the young *jinetera* who came to confirm
her presence at Sunday Mass, on his cell phone:

"Yudeysi, *mi amor,* I have to cancel the Mass on Sunday
because Italy is playing France. But come, the lot of you, to
watch the game with me. Your holy energy will perhaps help
the players from a distance, you never know: in this town,
anything is possible."

A bit embarrassed, the priest turns to you.

"What do you want me to do? You have to adapt to the
climate in which you live. You know Montesquieu's theories
on the relationship between climate and politics, in *The Spirit
of Laws*? All the Cubans' troubles are caused by too much
sun. It's starting to affect me, I admit. You can die from the
heat on Sundays in that crowded parish hall. No air conditioning, not even a fan. Besides, it's the World Cup! You have
to allow yourself a bit of pleasure now and then. And who
better than women to provide it to us, poor creatures at the
mercy of their bodies and their loves?"

During this time, Katia, another Caribbean goddess dressed
like a Tropicana dancer in high heels and a short, sequined
skirt, crosses the presbytery patio and enters the priest's office.
He, sorry at having to abandon us for an urgent confession,
asks us to return the next day and to spend the rest of our
stay with him. As you don't know how to say no, you promise
to return and go on with your passionate conversation. That

night, both of us have the same dream: the Holy Spirit as a splendid mulatta.

Two days before we leave Baracoa, there's a hurricane alert on Cubavisión, and you're delighted to see that your dream of living through a hurricane in the land of Fidel is going to materialize. We rush back to our hotel room to pick up what we need. I take my camera, and you, your paper and pastels. We make our way to the shelter to which we've been assigned, where an improvised fiesta is about to turn into a carnival. When we arrive, the place is already full to bursting. The electricity has not yet been cut, the air conditioning is working, and people are manoeuvring to get as close to it as possible because they know a hot night awaits us. Suddenly everything goes dark, and a cry of joy echoes through the shelter. No one seems surprised, or even fazed: since the Russians left, cutting the electricity at the end of the day has become one of the Cuban government's measures for managing its economy. The women light big candles here and there around this space that was once a military barracks. The drivers bring their flashlights, the nurses their emergency lamps from the hospital, and the party begins: we play dominoes, eat, dance, and talk politics, while an orchestra plays a frantic rhumba. No one seems to be worrying about the hurricane, everyone assumes things will end well. The hours pass, fatigue finally shows on people's faces, and sleep asserts itself. Like sardines, the people lie down in rows on the ground. As for you, you can't close your eyes on this euphoric day, with all your memories rising to the surface. You feel as if you're finally on familiar ground. You have a childlike air about you as you work away by candlelight, like painters from the past. While you paint, you talk.

"It's like back home, during the war, remember? It was so wonderful, that time in the shelters. We were all so close..."

"Papa, try to sleep."

"You know, I think I understand what bothers me so much about North America. It's the total lack of feeling close to other people. And also, the artificial light, everywhere."

"Go to bed!"

"Have you ever noticed that North Americans have a phobia of darkness? Have you observed that at night, in front of houses where everyone is asleep, there are always lamps lighting up the emptiness? That huge factories and office buildings stay lit all night even if no one's there? Everything, always, has to be lit up. Have you noticed that air conditioning is going full blast in empty hotels even in the middle of the desert? And that they waste the earth's energy by heating empty train stations that shut down at midnight? An advanced civilization that's so afraid of darkness and death!"

"Papa, you're disturbing the others!"

"They're all dead drunk. Let me enjoy the moment."

You cast your eyes admiringly over the room and its sleepers.

"You know, daughter, that's real life. Life without electricity, as in ancient times, when we were happy, lying one against the other. In America, everything is cinema, an image, it's all artificial, everything is perfect. Life is imperfect."

You show me again the sleepers huddled together, drunk and happy, while outside a violent hurricane is breaking windows, blowing off roofs, uprooting trees.

"Real life is being certain that if ever a sleepwalker were to leave this mass of people and disappear into the night, the person sleeping next to him would let everyone know. Try to wander off like that in North America. No one will look for you, and at dawn you'll only run into some Romanian or Mexican, grumpy and tired, hanging bags stuffed with advertising on people's doorknobs."

Five days later, we leave. Before taking the same *bicitaxi* driven by the same old man who'd been so astonished to see you pedalling along with him, you turn once more towards the Hotel La Rusa, as if to sum up the life of its illustrious occupant: "This woman travelled widely, most of the time in flight from the Marxist utopia. She ended up here, thinking to end her days as a rich heiress on a coffee plantation. But when the Cuban Revolution tolled imperialism's death knell on the island, she was smart enough to understand that no one can fight his own destiny. After all her wanderings, history caught up with her deep in a tropical forest. I think that, in the end, the goal of every life is to die in harmony with the spirit of one's time."

As we say farewell to the hotel staff, we see, hesitant and fragile, the silhouette of René, *la Rusa's* son, making its way in our direction. He holds out an envelope: "I think Mama had an affair with your President Tito when he visited our country. I found this photo among my mother's personal effects. I'd like to give it to your father."

The envelope contains a photo of Tito and Fidel sharing a cigar, probably taken during the Marshal's presidential visit to Cuba curing the 1970s. You're so happy to hold this unknown document in your hands that you embrace René several times to thank him for his kindness. To our great surprise, he knows the history of our country better than we do. I've never forgotten his words, which haunt me still:

"They seem very happy together, our leaders. Those visionaries forged the destiny of their people and of many generations to come. If Fidel had never existed, who would I be? A poor devil deferring to the laws of the marketplace and to the Americans? He was also a good man, your Marshal. But power always has its dark side. If Tito had never existed, would your father be such a sad man today? You have to be God to see these things clearly. In the meantime, we must, for the good of humanity, fight against injustice."

We're still pondering the old man's words when we land at the Santa Clara airport. You insist on paying homage to Che at the foot of his statue. Immediately afterwards we climb aboard a State taxi to head for Caibarién, where I hope to find the characters for my documentary. We drop our belongings at a *casa particular* near the Las Ruinas restaurant, actually built from real ruins, and that you find magnificent, with the orange and violet reflections on its faded facades. We leave immediately for La Isabela, a fishing village at the end of the world, where I've decided to do my research. To get to the village you have to take a bus to Sagua La Grande, a town burnt by the sun. All along the way, unrelenting signage greets intruders who have made their way into these remote parts. Fidel's slogans and citations line the walls: *Las ideas son únicas hijas de la revolución; Revolución o muerte!; La dignidad es el camino de la libertad* . . . An enormous portrait of Che stretches across structures that look like they once contained a thermal power station. Behind the rusted pipes of the abandoned factory, probably purchased from a European country, a *guajiro*, a peasant with a traditional straw hat, is working the soil with more energy than the oxen he's trying to guide. At Sagua, we're advised to take a *bicitaxi* to La Isabela, the last Cuban port and the launching place, past and present, for many illegal rafts headed to the United States. Our driver, a relatively young man, but one who has been worn down by the sun and a hard life, pedals haltingly while vaunting his country's social benefits. "Here we don't pay for medicine. It seems that where you come from, they invent sicknesses so as to operate on you and to make you pay more." He leaves us at Nueva Isabela, a phantasmagoria in the middle of nowhere. The buildings, of a brutalist ugliness inspired by Stalinist architecture, are lined up like dominoes. Later, we learn that these structures are made available free of charge to families that have lost their houses to hurricanes.

We climb on board a crowded *guagua* to get to Isabela. A deathly silence reigns in the little village's decrepit streets. The wooden houses all lean to one side or the other, depending on the humour of the hurricane. For there's been a stream of them; this year alone, the meteorologists foresee at least ten. The only windows that still have their panes are in what appear to be corner stores. Everything is sold there, but especially rum and sweets. The Cubans love little biscuits filled with cream. The wrapping seems to be the prime criterion in making one's choice, the more colourful the better. The road that leads to the point passes beside the port, which resembles a haunted film set. It's no longer in use, and even the water, elsewhere a turquoise blue, seems rusty in this solitary bay. The street bordering the coast is dotted with shacks that have been badly battered by the wind. Their doors are all wide open, and beyond them we can see the hands of ancient, benevolent women peeling garlic with an ear to their Brazilian soap operas.

The Caney restaurant, popular with the locals, serves fresh fish, very cheap, while the beer flows freely into the throats of fishermen come to enjoy their one day of rest. A man orders three platefuls, which he swallows down with gusto. Does he always have enough to eat? Can he often afford such a luxury? The restaurant gives onto the beach where weary fathers watch over their children in the water. They also keep an eye on unaccompanied women. A man with thick, square eyeglasses hums a *reggaetón* that echoes over the waves. Stray dogs, famished, come to sniff at empty cans, and then, forlorn, return to die in the shadows.

We get up from the table. I have no precise plan at Isabela, I want to check out the place and its people, to return later and write, or shoot a film whose subject still eludes me. This wandering about suits you fine, and while I take notes you draw what you see in front of you. Before moving on to a little bay where houses are suspended on stilts, we meet a gentle, fragile woman who is chopping up herbs and peppers. The sea comes right up to Mariza's house and sometimes flows into her living room, but this fisherman's wife makes little of it. On her walls are paintings of exotic landscapes:

snow-topped mountains, Niagara Falls, the Ardennes forest. Does she dream of travelling, even of leaving the island once and for all? As if she's reading my thoughts, she explains that, since the beginning of the revolution, it's from La Isabela de Sagua that most of the *balseros* leave. Only a few hundred kilometres from the Florida coast, its port marks the start of the shortest route for dissidents who want to reach the other side. The idea has certainly occurred to this fearful woman, but she would never dare put it into action. And then, would she know how to distinguish, among life's hardships, between the fate of fishing villages around the world and the result of the island's political situation? Her family seems to be one of the rare ones to have no members in the United States. For how long?

Leaving Martiza's house, we enter, like two intruders, the little nearby bay. There are five houses on stilts whose stair-cases, descending right to the water, also serve as a slide for the merry children who've had the good fortune to be born by the sea. A mother, a blonde woman who looks like a Swedish actress, is earnestly smoking a cigarette, the better to show off her nails, glazed with blood-red acrylic, and a lacy white overlay that might have enhanced the windows of her dream house. But Loyri has no more dreams. They've been swept away by the wind and the days that succeed each other with a monotony that anesthetizes everything. Her gaze empty, nonchalant, she doesn't seem touched by the country's political situation, and even less by the natural disasters that periodically engulf her house. Her arm rests on a bent knee, and she's wearing a red lace top together with velvet pants, unsuited to the climate, but resembling the form-fitting outfits of American film stars. Curiously, she doesn't offer us a taste of what makes for her livelihood. These shacks are in fact *paladares*, where you eat freshly fished lobster anointed with succulent garlic sauce. Is Loyri more preoccupied with the arrival of that white powder she's anxiously awaiting to allay her boredom? In her wistful contemplation of lives she will never live, the young woman betrays the uneasiness my questions cause her. How does she see the world? She was born and will probably die in La Isabela. In the meanwhile, life will run slowly, suffused with indolence.

We continue on our way, with the sense that there is only one thing certain about this bay, this place providence has forgotten: that the joy of young girls with bronzed skin leads inexorably to their mothers' despair. Yet you are dazzled by the simplicity of their lives, and you would like to stay there to capture it on your canvases. Like Gauguin, you'd like to render those orange shadows and blue hours. "What they don't know," you tell me, "is that happiness resides in the land of your birth and in eventless afternoons."

For once, we're on the same wavelength. On our way we meet an old man with a wrinkled face murmuring something in a barely comprehensible language, his syllables soaked in cheap rum. "Sancho Panza" tells whoever will listen that he has survived three major hurricanes, including that of 1933, one of the most violent the country has known. But in 1933 Sancho was not yet living in La Isabela. A native of Santa Clara province, this former policeman tells us proudly that he has spent his life in the service of his people. He knows his country well, and he's very proud of it, even if he admits how hard it is to survive on his pension of 200 pesos (17 dollars). He'd like to have a television set one day, but he's not fooling himself. There are no luxuries in his house, and all his possessions are hanging on a rope suspended in his windowless "living room": a t-shirt with holes in it, a plastic bag for shopping, and a pair of shoes in a sorry state.

He moved to La Isabela to find his children. His only daughter lives on the other side of the street and makes sure her father isn't carried off by the wind, or waves of rum. His son-in-law has applied sheets of metal strategically to parts of his house, but when the hurricanes bear down, there's nothing to be done. Why then insist at all costs on staying in this house that's really not a house at all? Sancho, despite alerts that follow in the wake of government orders to leave his house and go to a shelter, is unmoved. Like Santiago in Hemingway's *The Old Man and the Sea*, who battles the enormous marlin he will eventually dominate, he finds great happiness in the battle he's waging against the forces of nature. Is it recklessness, or the need to feel adrenaline in veins where his boiling blood once flowed? You, you understand him, you even endorse his resistance by pointing to yourself as a counter-example: "My biggest mistake was to leave my country when it needed me."

Carmen, Sancho's daughter, is a waitress at Tiburón, La Isabela's other restaurant. Most of the time, for lack of drinkable water, the only beverage available is Cristal beer or TuKola soda, a sort of tropical parody of Coca-Cola, less sugary and so less flavourful. Carmen is a woman around forty years old, a bit on the plump side. Her face radiates goodness and her seductive voice makes me think of perfume sellers in Canadian department stores. Her gaze, during our conversation, shifts regularly towards the sea, as if she were asking permission to tell us a secret. Carmen explains in her turn the human cost of the *balseros'* clandestine journey. I try to translate, but with a casual gesture you make me understand that it's not necessary, all the while keeping your eyes riveted on hers. Thousands of people have left the country from these shores situated less than 150 kilometres from Key West. This proximity in no way guarantees the success of the crossing: many *balseros* have perished on the high seas. You urge me to ask why these people risk everything to get to the United States. I translate for Carmen, who suddenly lifts her eyes to heaven and thanks it for having helped her brother to reach "the other side" safe and sound.

Carmen's mother has become seriously ill since the departure of her son. The long wait was very hard on her: eleven days with no news, eleven days without knowing if he'd perished or not. The parents have since divorced, Sancho Panza's alcoholism being the main cause of their separation. The brother has returned to his country twice since his exile. Carmen is very sad at the prospect of spending her life without him. For her, had the economic situation been different, none of this would have happened. You sniff: "So she mixes everything up! Economics and politics. The same bad luck that struck us will befall them one day!" I translate none of this for Carmen, but ask her, rather, how many of her fellow countrymen, in her opinion, have left Cuba for political reasons. "Very few," says Carmen, who is proud of the revolution's achievements. "You have to live through the hurricanes here to appreciate how the State helps us. The world has something to learn from us."

According to her, thanks to the State, when the hurricane season appears on the horizon, no villager has to fear for his or her life. Other than her *cabeza dura* of a father, she says loudly so he'll hear it at his table, everyone knows that all you have to do is follow the orders of the Civil Defence, and take refuge in shelters for the time required. During the last hurricane she had just undergone surgery and was bedridden. A special ambulance, there exclusively for cases like her own, came to fetch her and take her to the shelter. Carmen looks again at the sea. She starts to cry, forgetting for a moment that we're there. This woman, who suddenly seems to be bearing the weight of the world on her shoulders, leaves us to go and serve Sancho a TuKola and a dish of white rice and black beans, probably his only meal of the day. Suddenly, a heavy rain starts to flood La Isabela's streets. Waiting for our return *guagua*, you utter a few words that have remained lodged in my memory: "How many of Carmen's tears are in this deluge?"

Despite all the problems you glimpsed in Cuba, you refuse to accept the Western thesis that all communist systems are doomed to fail miserably. There is no perfect society, and, in your eyes, this little island has accomplished, at the cost even of its own well-being, the exploit of the century: resisting American imperialism. On the return flight you conclude the journey by applauding Fidel's successes: "He had to have real balls to overthrow a powerful enemy with a handful of guerrillas. But to bring down a regime is one thing, whereas to nobly hold out for half a century in the face of the greatest empire in the world, that's another. Say what you like, history will be on his side." I'd heard this refrain many times in the Yugoslavia of my childhood, but now that you've visited Cuba, your words have more weight. I'm starting to think that your admiration for the Cuban revolutionaries has unconsciously influenced me in my "type" of man. I'm attracted to tall, well-built individuals with hair like Che, the charisma of Camilo, and the stubbornness of Fidel. But above all, I'm attracted to men who view justice as the holiest thing there is. That's the moment you choose to whisper in my ear: "You must make children with a Cuban. In life you mustn't just fall in love with a man, lose your head like a donkey, and have children with him. You have to fall in love with a land, a culture, an identity. Can you imagine all that you'd be able to pass on to your children if their father were Cuban?"

Back in Ottawa, you repeat to whoever wants to listen that Cuba is a perfect society, paradise lost. No one takes you seriously, especially your nationalist friends who suffered under Tito. But for you, life is like that: "Some suffer for the cause; others, thanks to it, are happy." What counts in the end is the happiness you see on people's faces, and in Cuba, more than anywhere else, people seemed happy to you. The trip to Cuba has inspired you, but a new level of nostalgia has also come to veil your eyes. Since our return, you keep repeating that you want to follow the example of Sancho Panza: to end your life in a simple house, with no possessions but also the freedom to possess nothing. You want to be as free as a leaf in the wind, no longer hewing to the demands of daily life, but existing beyond the material world, far from any responsibility. You want to move on into an artist's ideal world, where all forms of constraint and prohibition are themselves prohibited.

For my part, I'm torn between the desire to help you follow your impulses, and sadness at seeing Mama bear her burden alone: paying bills, stocking the refrigerator, and ensuring that no one lacks for anything. She wears herself out in menial jobs that have nothing to do with her law degree. But unlike you, she's not ashamed of rolling up her sleeves and accepting contracts you regard as "humiliating," such as this job cleaning for a rich family in the upscale neighbourhood of Rockcliffe Park. And so she walks alone, before dawn, along the edge of their half-frozen private lake, into which she could have fallen a thousand times. I'm torn: must I go with you in search of your dreams, or be loyal to my mother, who stoops a bit lower every day under the weight of her responsibilities. Finally, I propose to help you find work because I know you won't do it alone: you don't even know the words you'd have to draw on for an interview. I answer the first ad I find seeking two people to work with the "*warms.*" I don't even know what that means, but I'm so anxious to help mother out that I don't take the time to reread the ad. We show up at a building on Bank Street where a man in his forties, large-stomached and with a reddish, greasy beard, asks us to lean over and familiarize ourselves with "the matter at hand." I bend to see what it is, and get the shivers. The ad didn't say "*warms,*" but "*worms*": thousands of wriggling earthworms waiting to be delivered to bait distributors. I turn around to see your face, but your thin silhouette is already across the street, cursing life, immigration, and the war: "I didn't save you from the war to cozy up to earthworms!"

The next day I answer another ad: "Peric Construction Inc." seeks handymen. I call and introduce myself in Serbo-Croat. I'm invited to appear for an interview the same day along with my father. You come unwillingly, because you want to paint and keep your feelings about Cuba alive. Dragging you away from your paintings pains me too, but the bills are piling up and Mama is at the end of her strength. In the bus that takes us to the offices of our potential employer, a combination of guilt and anger eats away at me. Our work consists of cleaning the debris left behind by workers in the renovation and demolition business. Old Peric's son speaks our language well, but he's married to a Canadian woman and is a perfect product of the American mentality: "*Time is money!*" We are to start the next day. I smile at him, shake his hand, and thank him, despite the paltry salary he's offering us, while assuring him that we'll be on time. Meanwhile, you're grumbling behind me like a child: "But . . . I'm not ready to start that soon, I have to prepare myself mentally, I've never done work like that." Leaving, I'm impatient to give Mama the news.

The next day we present ourselves at the address indicated by Junior: a Presbyterian church in the Sandy Hill neighbourhood. The Peric company is in the process of restoring the building's roof, and must rush to finish the work before Christmas. Our job consists of gathering up any discarded material we can carry in our arms. The work seems hard, but before starting we have time to acquaint ourselves with the place. You don't especially like religious buildings, but you admit to a preference for the Protestants' more restrained approach and decor. Inside, the church is austere, the only luxury being the cedar benches brought back from Lebanon by one of the faithful. No image or icon in the windows, and no gilded ornament, no metal other than the chalice that will receive the blood of Christ. With your half-broken reading glasses you carefully examine the Stations of the Cross that circle the church. I know you well enough to see that something isn't right. "This church needs to be restored inside, not outside." You approach each of the stations depicted in terracotta bas-reliefs. "It's badly done, because the artist produced the pieces first, then laid them into the wall. You can see the dividing line. He should have worked directly on the wall to make them continuous with the space. What's most bizarre is that the fourteenth station, the body of Jesus being placed in the tomb, is absent. That must be a blasphemy."

Someone behind us coughs. He introduces himself: the pastor. The man, thin and fair, seems intrigued. He asks me to tell you that he's impressed by your artistic knowledge and your propositions. "If he understood what I said, why is he speaking English?" The pastor continues to express himself in his perfect English. "Tell your father that I'm going to call Mr. Peric this very day and tell him I'd like to have your father restore the Stations of the Cross. We've been thinking about it for quite a while, but we've lacked the time, the means, and competent artisans. Your father seems to know what he's doing, and I think his presence here is a sign. If the restoration goes well, I'll entrust him with the fourteenth station, which I'd like to see completed before Christmas." When I translate the minister's proposition, you repress your smile, out of masculine pride. "Tell him that Christmas is in two weeks, and that he's asking me to perform a miracle." I see you're playing hard to get, but that deep down you're rejoicing at being offered, for the first time since the war, a job worthy of your skills. You're happy, too, at the sudden prospect of earning a good sum of money and contributing to the wellbeing of the family, which has been in survival mode since the start of the war.

On the first morning of our new job, the other immigrant workers, left at the site outside, look at us suspiciously, doubtless thinking that they, too, could have done the restoration. It's true that at first glance it doesn't seem difficult: you just have to reattach the bas-reliefs to the wall, create an impression of continuity, and polish the path that leads from one to the other. But you know the scope of the task at hand, and you ask the pastor for a key to the church so we can come and go at any time, and be sure that we'll finish the work on schedule. We work fourteen hours a day, and you've never been so happy. From time to time you lecture me, telling me that I ought to call Junior to negotiate our salary, make him understand that a job of this magnitude is worth thousands of dollars. But he never answers, and his secretary must try to reassure us in her charming Dalmatian accent.

Still, we continue to work very hard on the Stations of the Cross. Sometimes we even sleep in the church. With the cedar benches cracking beneath our tired bodies, we talk until the wee hours, sometimes about this and that, but more often about Jesus. I'm amazed by your knowledge of the Bible. You know each of the fourteen stations, and their different interpretations according to tradition, time period, and the beliefs of the popes. You even know the *Stabat Mater Dolorosa*, which accompanies the faithful when they stop at each station to pray and meditate on the Passion of Christ. You also inform me that the Stations of the Cross in the gardens of Saint Joseph's Oratory in Montreal are among the few that include a fifteenth station: the resurrection. We promise each other, once our work is finished—and our salary pocketed—to go there together to thank life for having bestowed on us, indeed, a feeling of resurrection. Sensing something in you that is much like piety, I can't stop myself from asking:

"But Papa, I thought you were Communist and anti-religious."

"I am, but that doesn't mean I have to be ignorant. Christianity is a pillar of our civilization. You have to force yourself to understand the origins of our collective unconscious. Now, Jesus and his suffering, and our guilt at having crucified a god, is all part of that."

"I don't remember Fra Ivan ever having spoken of Jesus in those terms in his catechism."

"I didn't know you'd taken a course in the catechism . . . Was it when your mother and I were separated from you? So tell me something, what did he say about Jesus? That the Son of God, incarnated in a man, sacrificed himself to redeem humanity's sins, and that we can go on sinning as a result?"

"Yes, more or less ... but not that we could continue to sin. I remember that I admired the heroic life and death of that man. I also liked that he could perform miracles."

"You were given the official version. But the true one, that of the historical Jesus and not the one co-opted by the Church, is that of a rebellious human being who wanted his fellow man to remedy a number of social injustices. He was neither a god nor a magician, just someone with a thirst for justice, a guerrilla fighter who dared to question the lies and laws that harmed the common people. He wanted to change the society in which he lived. That's all."

"That's already a lot. And so he sacrificed himself so that we might live in a better world."

"You have to stop presenting things in those terms! It's a way of seeing things that has spread like the plague through our collective unconscious."

"Can you explain to me your idea of the collective unconscious?"

"What I call the collective unconscious is a collection of ideas that manifests itself over and over again in the minds of an entire civilization. These ideas influence, without our being aware of it, our entire worldview. They are the threads from which it is woven."

"I have trouble following you. Where is Jesus in all that?"

Suddenly, you get up from your bench and light our work lamps, which we bought at a flea market from a disillusioned and alcoholic former filmmaker. You position yourself below the tenth station, Jesus nailed to the Cross.

"Look carefully at this scene. What do you see? What is reflected in the faces of these people, including Jesus?"

"Suffering and sadness."

"Is it normal for God to suffer so much? Is he not all-powerful? What is the message behind all that? That life is so hard that even God suffers? And what of us, then, the little people? What is our lot, we miserable mortals? If God is crucified, imagine what awaits us! That's one of the reasons Muslims consider it blasphemous to picture the divine. No image made by man, incomplete by definition, can represent the totality and infinity of God."

"But that's just the point. If the Son of God suffers within sight of all, it's because he's suffering for us, in our stead."

"That's too easy! And the corollary I detest is: sin as much as you want, it's not serious, because in any case God has redeemed all our sins! It's an act of irresponsibility and total inertia on the individual and collective level. This sense of defeat, of suffering, this crucifixion, this terrible putting to death in sight of all, the shamelessness of the wounded and degraded body, all that can be found deep in our collective unconscious. Instead of stimulating our minds with the concepts of vitality and virility, as did the ancient Greeks, for more than two thousand years we've been filling our heads with the image of a powerless man, dying in agony, without anyone coming to his aid. And in contemplating this same picture of suffering, we experience pleasure. The result is all this torment, repeating itself and increasing in cruelty day after day, century after century! We are far from being out of the woods. Terrible times are coming. And another world war."

I see your mounting anger. Your cheeks are reddening, and you don't know how to defuse the bomb in your breast. You rail against the weakness of Jesus, but in fact you're enraged at your own weakness. The one you don't want to address.

"But Fra Ivan said that in fact God had not abandoned Jesus, he'd only consented to let him die so that, through this terrible death, he might save humanity. Ivan also said that God had reserved the same fate for Saint Peter. Jesus' beloved disciple had denied him three times. Jesus had foreseen it, that's even why he'd been chosen. Because he knew that guilt, after his own death, was going to make Peter a better apostle. In fact, the outgrowth of his teaching and his redemptive faith enabled him to become a saint and to create a Christian kingdom on earth."

"And so you think the all-powerful God knew all that, and that he wanted Jesus to suffer? He could have got the same result another way, no? I don't believe in these fictions. The fifth utterance of Jesus on the cross, 'My God, my God, why have you forsaken me?' is the most perfect evidence for God's non-existence. There's nothing transcendent, no one behind the clouds. There's only matter and the strange accident of consciousness. Only the present moment, and life flowing in our veins. All the rest is well-packaged nonsense, designed to console us in our finitude."

I see, in listening to you, that where the Bible story is concerned you have the same contempt for Christ's blatant weakness as for his having been shamefully and barbarically put to death, a deed which no one tried to prevent.

The days that follow are deeply peaceful, thanks to the light and silence in the church, conducive to contemplation, and also to our feeling of accomplishment. You alternate your (almost) metaphysical lectures on Christ with long silences, during which we listen to the monotonous and restful cadences of the winds from the north. You're eager to finish the restoration of the first thirteen stations, and to begin work on Jesus' entombment. And then suddenly the church door opens and the voice of young Peric startles us both: "Good, I see you're making progress!" You quickly come down from your ladder and place yourself in front of your employer as if heading off a wild animal. "This is a sacred work site, be careful!" Peric shoots me a look, part startled, part mocking.

"There's nothing sacred but God!"

"My god is work."

"Exactly, that's why I'm here. My secretary says you want to talk to me?"

I try to insert myself into the conversation, but as Peric has chosen to speak in his native tongue, you take matters in hand.

"We've spoken to the priest who hired us. He knows this is an artistic project that must be paid at its true value."

"Obviously! Did you think I wasn't going to pay you?"

"I know you're going to pay us. But I want to know how much. As a matter of principle, the priest decided to pay you first."

"We already discussed your salary when you were hired: it's ten dollars an hour."

You laugh nervously.

"Is this some kind of joke?"

"No, it's not a joke. All employees start at the bottom of the ladder. Afterwards, if everything goes well, the salary gradually increases."

"But we're not like 'the other employees.' You have here two great artists capable not only of restoring religious works of art, but also of producing a made-to-order piece that harmonizes perfectly with the others!"

The tension rises. I pray to Jesus that Peric doesn't come out with something stupid yet again. But as he approaches the ninth station, the third fall of Jesus, he casts a disdainful eye over the work, and says, with the utmost nonchalance:

"Frankly, what you're doing is so simple that even a child could do it . . ."

Before he can even turn around you strike him with your fist. He drops like a stone and the back of his head hits the ground. You throw yourself onto him and administer two or three more blows. Arriving on the scene in a panic, the pastor tries to pull you apart. I cry out, not knowing who to help,

Peric bleeding on the floor, or you, who have just been deeply humiliated. You spit on the ground and leave, flinging off, in your own language, the worst curses you know.

Appalled by the situation, I approach Peric gingerly and apologize in your name before joining you outside. You stride towards the bus station, swearing that never again will you set foot in a church.

"And who's going to do the fourteenth station, papa? You can't leave like that. We have to finish the work."

"To be exploited by this vulture who's going to make a fortune off our backs? Never! You have to learn to be respected."

"And the entombment?"

"You'll finish it yourself, one day."

We've barely gotten down from the bus when a police car stops us. The policeman tells me that he's received an arrest order for aggressive attitude on a work site. He doesn't leave me time to translate. He goes up to you, determined to put you in handcuffs. You freeze for an instant, not understanding what's happening, but as soon as you see the handcuffs you start to run. The policeman, who looks like someone who spends a lot of time at the gym, quickly catches up and throws you down. Your face held to the ground, you struggle, and beg him to spare you this indignity in front of your daughter. I translate, weeping, while Mama and little brother watch the whole scene, powerless, from the balcony. You're led away handcuffed, and, avoiding my gaze, you look straight ahead. I'm frantic, worried about the prison conditions you're going to endure, the legal procedures, your claustrophobia, and all the bad memories that your imprisonment is going to revive. I beg the second officer to let me go with you. Nothing doing.

At home, we're all distraught. We call every contact we think might be able to help us. But America is not Europe, and we're recently arrived immigrants: our social network is tiny. Finally, after three days, you return. I see the same empty and defeated gaze you had after months in a concentration camp. On the succeeding nights you start to hallucinate, and the sinister spectacle of the war comes back into our lives in what we can as yet barely call our home. To find release from your psychic pain you start to drink, and we touch bottom along with you. The provisional peace our work in the church allowed us has vanished like a mirage, and the vicious circle of our afflictions closes in on us once more. As we await your trial, I beg you to return to your Cuban paintings, which you do. Several times a day I force you to look again at the photos we took, hoping that this suggestive technique will free you for a moment from the ghosts of the past. You paint, almost in spite of yourself, but every day you sink more deeply into the twin abysses of alcohol and depression. I sense that you're in the process of living out the last years of your life. Tacitly, a truth, unsummoned, reveals itself to me: powerless to help you succeed in your life, I will be there to help you succeed in your death.

THE FALL
OF THE TITANS

C UBA had a profound influence on your painting. The pastel colours, the mosaic of faces, the sun, the waves, the boats, the shells, a buoyant nature, Santería, the old American cars, the flowers that are born and die the same day, and above all the joy of the Cuban people. In the Chelsea Art Gallery at the foot of Gatineau Park, an Armenian friend has mounted an exhibition of your paintings called "Cuba, the Odyssey of a Dream." The English Canadians flock there like flies. A woman approaches you, saying she's fascinated by the way your eyes can find beauty even in a dictatorship. I translate, and you reply, "Madam, the place you're calling a dictatorship has made me believe that beauty can still save the world." While you busy yourself with your increasingly frequent showings, I try to complete my master's thesis. This minor fame you're enjoying isn't enough to relieve you of your profound heartsickness. You often come to slump down on my table, and, dead drunk, repeat like a parrot: "We have to find our island. We have to leave this continent."

I'm tired. My body is feeling the effect of six months at the hospital bedside of your cousin Semir, witnessing his strange dying off, which seemed to last forever. He understood neither English nor French, and even less the meaning of "pancreatic cancer." Before I explained it to him, no one had ever told him what this curious, banana-shaped organ was, nor where it was situated. I'm the one who delivered the diagnosis: the cancer was inoperable. I was the filter through which passed his fear, his pain, his vertigo, his humiliation, his indignation, his hope, his madness, and finally his regrets.

This high-achieving athlete, pride of the family, finally died at the age of thirty-nine. During the 1984 World Cup, he'd been part of the Yugoslav team. At the age of thirteen he became the idol of an entire city with the memorable header goal he scored when the Velež of Mostar were playing the Belgrade Red Stars. But he had left football far behind him in a country devastated by war and nationalism. To feed his family, he worked in a potato-chip factory. For some time, he'd been complaining of a pain in his back that all the doctors blamed on overworked muscles. When they discovered a serious cancer, you stopped talking for a week. You and Semir had spent many sleepless nights drinking and talking about your incurable *mostarghia*. You were comrades "from before the war," you hung out in the same places, and you had the same ideals. Every time the temperature dipped below zero, the Canadian winter plunged you deep into melancholy, and, lamenting your fate, you mourned the end of Tito's Yugoslavia and the good old days.

I'd never seen you so sad. When Semir died you shut yourself up in your room for three weeks, lying on your back, staring at the ceiling. You didn't even have the courage to go to the funeral. Semir had asked to be buried in his native land, begging his wife not to let him rot in the frozen Canadian ground. You had spared yourself his last days. I saw them through to the end, after his body had undergone that monstrous transformation which even Hollywood's best special effects couldn't have matched. His head had become the belly of a ray fish; only his terrified eyes, spread strangely wide, were there to remind us that he was still human. Overwhelmed, I was

witnessing the slow decline of a myth: Semir was my childhood hero, the perfect man, the generous cousin who looked
like Tom Cruise in *Top Gun*, and made all the girls dream.

The florist on Notre Dame Street, not far from the Lachine
Canal, swamped by the demand, called me twice a day to ask
what to write on all the bouquets being ordered from around
the world. My brain was no longer working; in his shop, I
stared at the flowers, trying to come up with a line or two,
but everything seemed futile next to the injustice of Semir's
fate. His last moments haunted me, and I resented the flowers for their beauty and light-heartedness. I tried in vain to
give some meaning to his story, and my philosophy thesis,
relegated to the back of a drawer, was of no help. Neither
Derrida nor Gadamer could cleanse my retina of those pic-
tures of a Titan's fall. You don't die of a stupid cancer at the
age of thirty-nine when you've been touched by grace and
escaped a massacre! It's an error in logic. I thought of the
ravenous eyes of this man who had not yet had his fill of the
sun; I thought of his friends who, like plants deprived of light,
would now wither away. I thought of his son, who was waiting
stubbornly, shut up in his room, shutters closed and eyelids
sealed, for the "Yugoslav style" football lesson his father had
promised him. A pillar of salt leaning on the florist's counter,
still waiting for an answer, I heard my telephone ring.

Your feeble voice at the other end of the line: "You're still
thinking?" How do you know? I realize once again that we
are connected by invisible threads, and this nearness frightens me. "Write this: Stars return to stars." The phone almost
drops from my hand. It's exactly right. You show me again
that you are poetry incarnate: deft and unpredictable, deep
and just. And it's often when you are most hateful that you
arrive to redeem everything, passing so close to the sun.

Semir's death robs me of any wish to complete my thesis,
which deals with otherness. Why would I need to write about

this abstract concept now that I've come to know the ultimate otherness, death? All the same, right after the funeral, morose and aggrieved, I decide to finish it. But there you are, again and again, intruding into my life, wanting me to translate something, to make you an appointment with the doctor, to buy something from your brother, to hold you by the hand. The very thought of translating for you now makes me feel ill. Translate, that's all I've been doing ever since I set foot on this earth. I am the one through whom the outside world reaches you. I receive information, I chew it up, and then, like a bird feeding its little ones, I regurgitate it gently into your mouth. Never two pieces at once, no food too tough or indigestible. And when, in my turn, I try to make sense of the world once night has come, your insomnia knocks at my door: "Why learn languages when no communication, ever, has been possible between men?" I struggle, body and soul, not to drown in the dark Balkan rivers that are your veins. One day, tired from bearing your world on my shoulders, I look you straight in the eye: "One of us has to leave so the other can live in peace." The equation is simple.

From that time on, as if you sense an end to your life, you become utterly unbearable. During your last year you lead a life of debauchery, where everything is permitted; you have no norms, no scruples. You drink until you pass out, you go into debt, you roll around on the ground in the middle of the street; you cry, you weep, you try to kill yourself. You steal from department stores for no reason, just like that, for the adrena- line. The next day you wake up with a hangover; ashamed and tinier than an ant, you apologize, vowing this will be the last time. But we all know that it's death that will one day decide to put an end to your depravity. Even after everything's over, I suspect your ghost of giving it the slip to prolong your Dio- nysian life in the beyond. I imagine you in Hell, perpetuating your Slavic self, somewhere between the burlesque and the tragic, between white and black, between laughter and tears.

I told you one day that it was either you or me, that I felt as if I'd lived a thousand years; I was exhausted by the dizzying gymnastics of your tragic soul that never came to rest. I had begun to dream of inner peace. I arranged things so as to continue my studies in another city, two hundred kilometres from yours. Since the war, we'd been living crammed in a caravan with no brakes, reeling towards disaster. I needed distance in order to try to become a "normal" adult.

It's also your fault that I found myself in the clutches of philosophy. The first time you talked to me about it was on my eleventh birthday. At the foot of the Karaberg mosque, which provided, according to you, "the coolest shade" in Mostar, a bit tipsy and exalted by the incomparable beauty of our little city, you introduced me to philosophy without suspecting that my soul would be steeped in the rapture of its sages for all time. What remains with me from this first lesson is the crystalline certitude that, in our universe, all is implicit in all, and that it's impossible to conceive of one thing without thinking about all the others. I follow your instructions to the letter, and I experience the pantheism of Spinoza and Plotinus in everyday life: the exalted and hyperactive child I am feels herself in symbiosis with the beauty that surrounds her. I am the voice of the muezzin who calls to prayer, the Neretva that hurls itself into the sea, the insistent carillon of the Franciscan church, the wind from the south, the cherry trees in bloom, the paving stones of the old city, the houses of the poets, the heat of the night. And so, it's thanks to you that today I am pursuing my profession as a teacher of philosophy. For me, there's no occupation more gratifying than igniting the flame that is a passion for ideas in the eyes of young people. Had it not been for the century-old tradition of architecture in your family, you might perhaps have become a philosopher yourself, contemplating life and humanity from afar. For it's only from a distance, you used to say, that it's possible to get a sense of the whole. But you were never truly contemplative; when you've grown up in the shadow of Roma caravans, you remain forever a worshiper of Dionysus.

And so I leave the family home to find refuge in Montreal. After the maelstrom of the war, exile, and your internal struggles, I just want to be at peace and to be responsible for no one. Despite your bohemian nature, the patriarchal tradition from which you have sprung forbids you from letting a "girl" fly off on her own wings in this way.

"Papa, I just want to write my thesis in peace!"

"Fine, as long as I'm there."

I fight for air. I suffocate. I'm drowning in your constant presence. I dream of silence. A monastery. An order of some sort. Decades of wordlessness. Silent shadows. Prayer. Rigour. The Carthusians? It doesn't matter, but let it be far from the Balkans and their powder keg, far from you and your tireless, insatiable Slavic soul. For the first time, I dare to say no to you. "If you come, my door will be closed." You don't reply. I hear the telephone drop. Mama screams. Brother panics. I'm powerless and terrified at the other end of the line. I cry: "Mama, what's happened?" No one answers. I rush off to Ottawa. Mili calls me along the way. "Papa's in the hospital, he's jumped from the balcony." Excuse me? I explode with laughter just as I'm bursting into tears. A joke? No. I know it's serious, because that's just like you. I know you did it.

Three hours later, I'm at the hospital. You've fractured your ankle and heel. From behind the curtain you curse Canada, capitalism, and the feminism that have stolen your little girl, your treasure. The nurse comes into the room for the nth time. With no explanation, she orders you to stretch out and gets ready to take your measurements. You get even more furious. "Why is she measuring me, that one?" Good

question. Does she know herself? We laugh, despite the tragedy of the situation.

Your six months of convalescence are a relief to us all. You stay
quietly at home and I at last make progress on my thesis, even
if I haven't had the heart, after that drama, to leave for Montreal. "What's the point, doing a thesis in philosophy?" you ask
me one day. "Philosophy is for people who have never lived.
You, you could give them lessons in survival, all those uptight
professors!" I try to explain to you that philosophy helps me
to free myself from the vortex in which I've found myself,
despite my best efforts. "Impossible, my dear. The vortex will
suck you down in the end. Have you not learned your Hera-
clitus? The only thing you can do before you're finally swallowed up is to dance and sing, like the Roma." You have a gift
for deconstructing my every effort. And as soon as your heel
and ankle start to get better, you again begin to navigate the
Bermuda Triangle of your soul, and gone is the modicum of
peace we've been accorded since your fall. Each day, you drag
us a little farther down into the abyss.

    Summer is hot and humid in the Canadian capital. The
wealthiest leave the city. Some return to their native country
on the other side of the great sea, others drive to cottages
on one of the many Canadian lakes. We don't have enough
money to cross the ocean, and even less to rent a house on
a lake. You're not working. Mama scrapes up a few dollars
here and there. Mili plays football, and me, I'm a waitress at
National Arts Centre banquets, where a clan of Portuguese
have taken over the catering service. The boss can't stand me,
in his opinion all Yugoslavs are full of themselves. I serve veg-
etarian dishes to hockey players' scrawny wives. They all have
the same pair of silicon breasts, the same diamonds around
their necks, and the same Hollywood smile, followed inexorably by a full-throated *Oh my God!* Our two salaries aren't

enough to allow us to go away, but for all that, you don't stop hammering away at the importance of taking vacations and returning to one's own country. Assuming a pose worthy of Captain Cook at the prow of his ship, you proclaim, for the hundredth time in thirteen years, the sentence that set us off on a clandestine journey across the earth. "Let us leave, the sea is fine." But we are no longer in Europe, and we can't just go through customs and find ourselves once again, in the time it takes to visit a museum or to munch a croissant, in Holland or France. We're in America, and America is huge. It's so huge it gives you vertigo. "Here, the problem is that there's no centre."

In fact, the centre has shifted since we pulled up anchor on the Adriatic coast. The centre now is us, and we are at home as long as we have a body. Everything else is outside. Foreign. Since Semir's death, I try to make you understand this intuition I have: man's only country has as its frontier the fragile membrane that is his skin. You think I'm reciting a philosophy lesson I've learned in a lecture hall. "No, Papa, listen to me: the day we have no more country is when our body shuts down, when our blood stops circulating, and when we take on the colour of ash, when our breathing stops forever, and when we're placed in the bottom of a coffin." But you don't listen. You keep drinking and smoking like a chimney and I'm afraid for you. "Let us leave, the sea is fine," your keep repeating during this stifling summer. But leave for where? Where do you want us to go now? To your home? But it doesn't exist anymore, and you yourself admit it. You'd like us to move to Cuba, to buy a house on the coast, and live on fish and tropical fruits. That's a fine dream. But you don't listen when we explain that no foreigner can stay in Cuba for more than six months. And then, you don't ask Mama's opinion, and you refuse to understand that Mili and I, we want to decide for ourselves.

Worn out by your existential restlessness, we just want to settle down somewhere. We'd like to become citizens of a country, with papers in order and our civil rights recognized. Unanimously, in front of a rerun of *Who Wants to be a Millionaire*, that American program we hate but watch anyway, the family council votes down your fantasies. When you see that no one is paying any more attention to you, you go out onto the balcony and light a cigarette. Paco the cat, "the love of your life," the only being that understands you, goes with you. I hear you murmur something. I turn to see what you're doing. You're lying down on the balcony and talking to Paco: "When I leave this world, all my wealth, it's to you I'll leave it, since you're the only one who loves and understands me." What wealth? "Papa, you're hallucinating, it's hot, come back in." Our eyelids weighed down by the heat, we're half asleep. You take advantage of our negligence to wind the metal cord hanging from the balcony door around your neck, and, in a sudden move, overturn the plastic chair.

We end the day at the hospital. As usual, I translate an account of your existential angst for the psychiatrists. Everything is tragic and everything is funny. Everything is strangely unreal. Like this observation by Mama: "You chose a good day to do that. You saved us from the heat wave. At least there's air conditioning here. Next time, choose another hot day." Mama. Mama's words to put things in order. In our family, Mama represents reason, trustworthiness, responsibility. In our family, Mama is Papa and Papa is Mama. Since the beginning of the war, she's had to take your place, and attend to our needs all on her own. This arduous task has merged with her complex personality. She doesn't like showing her emotions. For her, it's a weakness. Is that why I've always been closer to you, and why this book is entirely devoted to you? The war, our being uprooted, and all the tragedies we've seen and lived through, you responded to them with your feelings. Only later did I come to understand that one could also face life with reason. If I am first and foremost my father's daughter, someone who draws on a grid of feelings to understand the world, our "pocket of survival in times of crisis" was a creation of Mama and myself, and it overshadowed the mother-daughter bond, which is emotional by definition. During all those years, my mother was a reliable associate. I learned that I had a mother, a person with feelings, on the day of your death. When we all gathered at your bedside, she, who had not shut her eyes for several weeks, suddenly crumbled, as if her mask had shattered into a thousand pieces. Your disappearance heralded the emergence of a new relationship between us, the most complex one there is, in my opinion: that of mother to daughter. But that's for another book.

For now you are alive, and we have to deal with your fragile mental state and your next suicide attempt. Because it's not long in coming. A few months after a cure for alcoholism and a failed therapy, you're saying again and again that every psychiatrist needs a psychiatrist, and that the planet is an open-air asylum. And then, realizing the futility of your mantra, "Let us leave, the sea is fine," you perform the same despairing ritual. They say that a true suicide rarely repeats the same act twice, and that he contrives, in order to avoid the shame of another failure, to leave this world once and for all. But here you are, with your third attempt. It's become a fishy business.

When it happens, brother is playing football in front of our building's garage in the Bayshore neighbourhood. No one is playing with him: in North America, suburbs are not as animated as in Europe. I'm reading in the bedroom while Mama, wearing her mudpack, is reading *Gloria*, a sort of Croatian *ELLE*, on the Internet. She's appalled by the insipid, anaemic beauty of the new Miss Universe, while lamenting the true beauty of the women of her time. So as not to disturb her pack, she mimes the curves, the legs, the soft white skin, and the heart-shaped mouth of Gina Lollobrigida.

Mama was chosen Miss Herzegovina in 1978, and her beauty afforded her a few newspaper articles, to the great annoyance of her older sister, who had two plump daughters with moustaches. As her mudpack has dried, she can barely open her mouth. "You look like a talking statue," I tell her, before rereading the same sentence by Heidegger for the fifth time. Suddenly we hear the dry sound of the balcony chair tipping over. Mama doesn't move, despite Paco's meowing for help. Still focused on her mask, she asks me, almost casually: "Will you go and see if your father is still alive?" On the balcony you've once more made a spectacle of yourself, trying to take your own life. We're desperate. We don't know what to do with you anymore, nor do you. We can read the despair in your eyes. You want to get back to your *baraka*, your cabin, to die in peace. You beg: "I've had enough of foreign places. Let's go back home ..." But you know perfectly well that your country, officially, no longer exists, and that Cuba isn't awaiting you with open arms. All you know for sure is that America is not for you. You keep on saying: "If I spend another winter here, I'll die." You want to go back to Mostar, but only with us. But this "us" is trying to embrace new rules to lead a normal life. This "us" is undertaking, for better or worse, the imposition of certain limits, without which it knows it will not be able to survive. Since the day when the absurd worked its way into the farthest corners of our eccentric lives, only a monotone, dull, and routine existence can afford us a certain respite.

That calamitous summer is coming to an end, but bad news continues to befall you. One after another, two of your best friends have departed this world. One died of a heart attack, the other of a strange leukemia. You're like a fish out of water. We now know how helpless you are, faced with loss and mourning. The only way for you to deal with the pain is to drown yourself in alcohol, and we fear a relapse. To our surprise, you don't opt for the bottle, but for a box of painkillers. You complain of back pain behind your ribs. "That's from my fall, I know," you say. You treat yourself on your own until the end of September. But it gets worse. You have to go to the doctor, everyone says so, but you, stubborn, refuse. You only decide to do so in the month of March. The X-ray worries the doctor, who draws a circle around a spot with a red felt pen and appends a single adjective: urgent. The day we're told you have a mass on your lung, Ottawa is abloom with the multi-coloured tulips whose bulbs the Queen of the Netherlands ships to Canada every year by the thousands. The tradition dates from the end of the Second World War, a gesture of gratitude for the role Canadians played in the Netherlands' liberation, as well as for the sanctuary accorded Princess Juliana and her children during the war. Even now, for me, the shape of a tulip reminds me of your cancerous tumour. It's a flower that I find terribly ugly. You guess from my trembling voice that something is amiss. You prefer to talk about the tulips. "The Dutch are grateful to the Canadians for having liberated them from the Nazis. And we, how did we thank Tito for saving us from fascism? Instead of flowers, we sent bombs."

The very day of your diagnosis, I receive a letter of invitation from the Sorbonne. A professor has agreed to supervise my doctoral thesis. I've saved up for years to this exact end. Paris is at last at my beck and call, and I'm told on the telephone that my father has a mass "as large as a newborn's head" on his right lung. We go to the hospital. Your illness is made in your image: aggressive, headstrong, and fierce. An immense seventeen-centimetre tumour has invaded your entire lung. I translate. You doubt the competence of the Canadian doctor. "Tell him he's wrong. It's impossible for me to have a cancer: I was the best footballer in town." I want to cry out: "What does that have to do with it?" You've smoked like a chimney, day and night, for thirty-five years, up to three packs a day. And yet I don't want to believe it either. I'm more afraid than you are. When I tell my friends about it I tremble at the idea of your death, and my language betrays me. I confuse *utopia*, a word that resembles you so, with biopsy, or perhaps autopsy. I say they're going to have to do a *utopsy*. I hold you by the hand and outline the sequence of events that, like a cascade, will succeed each other with implacable logic. Even without cancer you're already fragile, weakened by life, long depressions, alcohol, exile, the loss of meaning in your life, and disenchantment. I carefully chew up the doctors' words before regurgitating what they have to say. Mama recommends that I not translate everything. You won't be able to bear it, she thinks. "You have a mass on your right lung that looks like an infection. They're going to have to take it out. It's nothing serious." You believe this version only halfway.

In fact, we don't yet know if you're a good candidate for the surgery. In front of the little Afro-Cuban altar that, before your sickness, was just a decorative object in my little blue bedroom, blue like the Caribbean, I pray for good news. The Orishas, gods of Santería, seem to have heard me. It appears that those elder sons of the Creator, Olodumare, are responsible for, among other miracles, Fidel's longevity. After an interminable series of tests, including a dozen confinements in scanners, we learn that, to the obvious surprise of the entire medical team, your mass is stagnant, and that there are no metastases. You're the perfect candidate for the excision, and you have one chance in two to survive. We scream with joy, but you're not impressed. We think the operation frightens you. But we learn rather quickly that your existential dilemma has nothing to do with your fear of the knife or of death, but rather resides in the gender of your surgeon! It's a woman, and you want nothing of it. You can't put your life in the hands of this little girl!

Short and slight, with cropped hair and intense green eyes, your surgeon carries her thirty years with authority. Her voice is hesitant, and she repeats herself often, as if to be sure that her words really are reaching the eardrums of those she's addressing. When she isn't smiling, her face is a picture of cold, impersonal science. And yet as soon as the muscles in the hollows of her cheeks contract, she becomes human, and is transformed into a beautiful woman. Very soon you're doing everything you can to make her smile. Despite the language barrier inherent in your relationship, which ought to consign you to silence, the doctor seems to be the only person who understands you. She often comes to see you, places her hand on your knee, and talks to you in French as if it were the most natural thing in the world, as if you understood everything. "*Ça va les médicaments? C'est bon comme ça?*" You answer, returning her smile. "*Oui, c'est bon comme ça.*" Your sexist prejudices vanish as soon as she crosses the threshold of your room, and everyone can see that you're her pet. She's even allowed Mama to sleep at your side. Your doubts about her disappear for good the day you learn that, not only does she, like you, have a twin brother, but that she has just given birth to twins. Twins are special in your eyes, in that they are by definition immune from this flaw you despise so much: individualism. You've always been prone to these theories that astonish, but which, in their spontaneity and frankness, impose a certain legitimacy. And so you accept the operation because your surgeon is a twin.

Every night after work I go to see you. You're my breath of fresh air after monotonous, suffocating hours with the highly placed Canadian bureaucrats to whom I teach French because they must learn the other official language of our great bilingual country if they want their careers to advance. Set beside your imminent death, the questions to which they have to reply in French, exasperate me: "Do you think Canadian bilingualism is a political initiative? What do you think of the fiscal imbalance between the provinces? What will happen to the Canadian government after the departure of the baby boomers? Does creativity have a place in the public service?" Their grating accents continue to echo in my ears after work, but dissipate as soon as I see you. You're telling everyone that you'll soon be returning to Mostar. You'll be there for the cherries, and you'll begin, as soon as winter arrives, to look for a stone house in the south of France. Your travels will, from that time on, know only one itinerary: Herzegovina to Provence. You insist that you're not unreasonable, you just want a little farmhouse with a barn and some animals—because you want to raise chickens and goats. In your dreaming head, the house is surrounded by an immense field of lavender. Moving aside the tubes protruding from your arms, you draw the house, the barn, and the lavender on a piece of paper. You have total confidence in your fictions, and only today do I understand the source of my own propensity to fantasize.

The operation lasts ten hours. Every time she takes a rest, your surgeon comes to see us in the waiting room to reassure us. At ten minutes before midnight, she at last comes out of the operating room. "Everything went well. I'm very satisfied with your father's condition. On the other hand, I have to advise you that something very rare happened. When we opened the thorax and began to remove the mass, there was an upsurge of blood in the body. It's as if the whole region were suddenly immersed, we don't know why. . . We do everything we can to avoid this, but unfortunately, it sometimes happens." We know what that means: some cancerous cells may have escaped from the tumour to flow elsewhere through your body. And that's exactly what happened. Four weeks after the operation, you begin to feel pain again, this time emanating from your neck. The region is scanned, and it's found that the cancer has taken up residence in your spinal column. According to the statistics, you only have six months to live.

You spend your days between the house and the hospital, and you accept the chemotherapy treatments because you want to heal and turn the page on your past. "I want to start a new life, between France and Herzegovina. All I'll be lacking is a little Maya to teach to swim." I'm also persuaded that, if you come through, things will be different. One day I realize that you're not the man I knew. Your beard long, your gaze dark and hollow, you seem to be grasping the reality of your illness for the first time.

"I'm at the end of the line."

"You're invincible, Papa, don't worry."

"*No one is invincible!*"

The patient sharing your room has given me a start. He's speaking in Serbo-Croatian. His name is Slobodan, and he too is walking on the edge of a precipice. "*Ovaj rat nas je sve posekao.*" He has a Serbian accent, from Belgrade, that you've always loved. You repeat his words: "The war did us all in . . . He's right." Suddenly, you turn to me. "Don't come back to see me. I've nothing more to give you, no more idiocies to relate." I look out the window. Everything would be so dreary without "your idiocies." We think we live in hell with the people we love, but it's when they threaten to leave us that we get a glimpse of what hell really is. You still have dreams to share, laws to circumvent, and borders to cross in secret. You'd still need hundreds of sleepless nights to talk to me about our Titoist childhood, when you were "the happiest person in the world." You still have so many myths to destroy, so many canvases to paint, so many minds to convert to your philosophy of the moment. "Arrange to leave this continent, or I'm going to have to, even after my death, find a Ulysses to lead you to safe harbour." And where will this harbour be, Papa? The little girl in me bursts into tears. "Stop saying silly things, Papa. You know that if you die, I will too, I'll die with you." Suddenly, time stops. The old light appears in your eyes. For so long, that's what you've been waiting for: an absolute declaration of love. For years we've been playing at cat-and-mouse, not saying what counts. You seem to be breathing easier. "Go and get us a coffee, the blackest possible." You only drink black coffee, pure and bitter, like life.

"And your philosophy, how is it going?"

"I'm staying here. I've transferred my doctorate to the University of Ottawa."

A Catholic priest enters the room. He's happy to meet me. "People are talking about you. I was anxious to meet this child who is sacrificing so much for her parents. That's rare, these days." While he's being courteous, you're charming the Haitian nurse who has come to take a bit more of your blood. No one understands how, despite your linguistic handicap, your charisma charms all the women who come near you. The priest wants to know, in case something happens to you, if you want to receive the last rites. I know I can't translate such a monstrosity. I reply in your stead:

"You know, he's a communist."

But the priest doesn't let go:

"I too was a communist. In Rwanda, before the barbarians massacred thirteen members of my family before my eyes. Only my faith saved me."

What to reply? How not to offend him? You're becoming impatient. You raise your hand and say to the priest: "Me tired, me need to sleep, you go away please." The advantage of speaking no language is that you can reduce communication to its essentials. The priest excuses himself and leaves the room. It's the moment you choose to give me the most useful lesson of my life: "Don't let yourself be infected by the disease of Western political correctness. When someone or something is tiring you out, set a limit right away. Even in conversation, a quick, clean death is better than a slow decline."

Cut off from the outside world and the codes that regulate it, you've always operated beyond culture. You live in an instinctive, almost primitive world, where everything answers to the laws of survival: kill before being killed, eat before being eaten. It's to this savage solipsism that you owe your capacity to seize on the essence of people, to sense at once what they're made from. That doesn't always suit me, especially when, seduced by masks and frills, I surround myself with people whose soul is stamped with the seal of dissimulation, or an invisible psychic unease. I've sometimes wanted to bang my head against a wall when, as I'm in a rush, all excited, to introduce you to a new boyfriend, you've casually turned your head in our direction, and spat out the following words: "Another jackass! Why are you always introducing me to these jackasses? It's in Cuba that you'll find him, your warrior!" You always had this gross and pitiless way of judging people. But every time subsequent events proved you right, and after many evasions, I came to the same conclusion: another jackass. "My daughter, it's a Caesar that you need. A Caesar for a Cleopatra." A thousand times I heard this phrase from your mouth, which said sweet things only about me. It was a way of keeping me only for yourself, that I admit. But it instilled in me a certain assurance that perhaps attracts men with a warrior allure, who believe Helen's abduction was a legitimate reason to wage war on Troy.

Between two hospital stays, you enjoy the "house." I notice that, for the first time in ten years, you seem to appreciate this apartment and feel at home there. We watch CNN while cursing the stupidity of Bush junior. In your moments of anger, you love repeating the Serb slogan from the time of the 1997 American bombings: "Christopher Columbus, son of a whore!" Paco curls up at your feet. Your charisma even charms cats. I'd like to talk to you, but my chin is trembling. I don't know where to begin. You speak first. "Mayita, my love, I apologize for all the hard words and insults I've addressed to you. Some of my letters are proof in writing that you have every right to deny me publicly. But do not do it. They were the words of a drunkard. You are the light of my life. My oxygen and my reason for being." Suddenly you start weeping like a child. I do too, obviously, and Paco mews along with us. During this time the television is transmitting images of Iraqi mothers trying to extract pieces of their offspring from Baghdad's ruins. That day, everything becomes crystal clear. You apologize to Mama also, and to little brother, and then you spend a week crying on the sofa, asking yourself why you made our lives so impossible, as if war, exile, hiding, uncertainty, and fear for the future weren't enough. Why did you not appreciate the peaceful mornings in all the countries where we lived? This error haunts you, now that the shades are lying in wait.

I find it hard to bear my own helplessness when faced with your pulse, slowing with each beat, your yellowing skin, the shadows under your eyes, greyer each day, the odour of your body, which is breaking down like an overripe fruit. Above all there is the fear, this invisible thread that runs through every cell, every molecule, every atom of your body, and cries for help. Your breathing is becoming more and more difficult. I suffocate for you. As fear and death take hold, your once imperious demands melt away like the walls of a sandcastle at high tide. I feel, tacitly, that you are proving me right: the body is our only native land. Your growing self-awareness is accompanied by the expression of deep and authentic desires, probably because you feel these will be your last. Thus, you are dying to see your sister, Jadranka, again. You were very close in adolescence and during much of your adult lives, and she remains, in your eyes, the only woman capable of understanding you. You've even convinced yourself that, if she comes, you will be cured. But she refuses to come to see you. Croatia is far away, and she doesn't see what her visit would change. I think of Levi's book, *Christ Stopped at Eboli*. When the protagonist's sister comes to visit him in the remote town of Gagliano, the peasants suddenly look at him with admiration because he has a sister, and to have a sister is to enjoy the privilege bestowed by blood, which confers that sacred and mysterious sense of an affinity that goes beyond words. In archaic thought, the fraternal bond is the strongest there is. If this feeling is not entirely shared by your sister, your brother, on the other hand, has kept alive the sacred fire of twin-ship and fraternity. Some time after you, my uncle suddenly dies, leaving behind him a heartbreaking note: "I am leaving because I do not know how to live without half of my self."

The doctors have let you go home. But you feel so sick that no sooner have you crossed the threshold, we have to call an ambulance again. You're weakened and terribly thin. The paramedics decide to drive you to another hospital in the capital, which doesn't know your case. In the ambulance, you ask me to help you realize a scheme. "As they don't know me, we won't tell them I've been operated on. You'll see, they won't even notice I've lost a lung." I pretend I'll say nothing to the doctors, even though you'd have to be blind not to be struck by your cancerous appearance. I have in my pockets your favou-rite cakes, which you start to chew every time the nurse comes to give you a needle. While you're chewing, Doctor White puts into words, for the first time, a verdict we know perfectly well.

"*I think your father is dying.*"

"What, what's she saying? Why is she talking in English? Translate for me!"

"Nothing important, just a little infection. It will pass."

I clench my teeth so as not to burst into tears, and tell myself that you can't die today because mules like you don't die. You see the expression on the face of the young doctor, and insist that you be taken to a hospital "where they speak French!," as if the truth, in French, would be less painful. We head for the hospital that's treating you, in Gatineau. You ask to see *your* doctor, the short, slight surgeon so familiar with the world of twins. For the first time she doesn't smile on see-ing you. She talks to me as if you and Mama were not present:

"Your father is dying."

"*Votre père est en train de mourir.*"

You're right, the sentence is gentler in French. However, Mama asks me not to translate, even if you know perfectly well why you're being assigned to the palliative care floor, the one you call "the floor for war prisoners." You're failing fast. You seem to age ten years every minute, and I pray to heaven you'll be spared Semir's long decline, and above all the alteration that left him unrecognizable. After one week, you've lost all independence. I put your arms around my neck and I lift you to make you walk. I want to be a crutch for your body, as I was your crutch for language. I want to be the woman *by your side*, as in that new translation of the Bible that I would find in Split after your death. You are beyond exhaustion, and yet you seem very happy to be with me. With a last effort of will, you agree to take one final walk. I slide myself under your right shoulder. The operation's terrible carnage has carved a huge hollow into your chest, and your arm, suspended in air, makes me think of one passenger too many strap-hanging on an overcrowded train in India. You're like a wounded bird trying to fly, in spite of everything. Your movements are uncoordinated, you stumble constantly, and yet you smile, looking me straight in the eye, as if to distract my gaze from that hole of which you are ashamed. To reassure you, I hold you tightly against me, while you, you try to amuse me: "Remember the Russian corset we brought back from Baracoa? Do you think it would look good on me and hide the hole? We should try it."

A little later, you fall into a semi-coma. Euthanasia isn't yet officially allowed in Quebec, but the doses of poison the palliative-care doctors administer to the dying are a form of assisted death. The doctor responsible for the floor, clearly aware of my appeals to the orderlies, comes to see me. Our tense exchange takes place while you are apparently at rest in a peaceful sleep from which you will only wake to babble some final prophecies, such as, "The island is sinking in flames in the middle of Lac Léman."

"Who gave you permission to kill him?"

"If I stop administering opioids to your father, he'll suffer terribly."

"Stop! He's agreed to nothing!"

I want you to come back to yourself and to decide on your own. The doctor takes my demand very seriously: he drastically diminishes all the analgesics. The effect is felt a few hours later. You are breathing with such difficulty that I can hear your groans as I'm coming out of the elevator. Every breath is the meagre booty from a terrible battle. "Give him back the same doses. I don't want him to suffer."

You breathe your last near dawn. As we enter your room, Mama collapses. Seven years later, she still hasn't recovered. It's little brother who is her crutch. To each his lot.

In Mostar, hundreds of people come out to attend your funeral. I am staggered by the size of this gathering, which confirms for me that you never stopped belonging to this place. I meet your childhood friends again. I've heard nothing of them since the war, not even if they were alive or dead. By their very presence, they awaken my faith in life's continuity, and lessen one of my greatest fears: that of finding myself alone, or surrounded by strangers, when placed in the earth. "To belong" wasn't in my vocabulary before the day I saw that long procession paying homage to you as "a child of this land." Seventeen years have passed since you left. But on your childhood ground the bonds remain, tribal and sacred. In a cemetery where none of your precursors were interred, who would have come to bid you farewell?

As I read the quiet stoicism inherent in ritual on people's faces, thoughts of another order are dancing in my head. They must be the result of the Lexilium, this powerful anti-anxiety medication my aunt gave me "so as not to pass out." Behind my large, dark glasses, I stand timidly beside the coffin. It's very hot, and yet there's cold sweat creeping down my back. The apparent calm of my face masks my suppressed emotion, ready to burst out. I reason with myself: it must be the fatigue, the bureaucracy, the sleepless nights, the anxiety, and also the material reality of your death embodied in this ceremony. Suddenly, I recognize Beli, your childhood friend, your faithful companion when you were just entering into life. You were inseparable for almost forty years. You shared everything, including Milica, a lethal beauty who turned your head just before you left the city in the wake of a banal incident not unlike many others on the plains of Vojvodina. Your friendship with Beli was imbued with harmony, mutual respect, and boundless tenderness. Your one quarrel was caused by the war. You didn't want to take up arms for anything in the world, while Beli wanted to defend "his territory."

As soon as he sees it, Beli throws himself on the coffin and wraps his arms about it, as if through his embrace he could touch you one last time. The charm of Slavic men resides in the gap between their day-to-day nonchalance and their passion in chosen moments. Beli cries like a child. He cries, he shouts, and he begs life to give him back his brother: "Why did you go so far? I told you, the sun over there is not the same sun. And me, now, what am I going to do without you? Seventeen years I wait, and you come back to me like this, stretched out and silent! You can't do this to me, Nenad, you can't. Please get up, I want you to taste the grappa I make myself, with a little white cheese I bought from the peasants. You remember the old man who lived alone in the mountains? Well, he's still with us in this world! You know what saved him? Mostar's sun!"

While Beli is chanting his hymn to friendship, I'm suddenly distressed at not having known a bond like yours in my own life. I have many friends, certainly, but the scene I'm witnessing proves to me that childhood friendships are the solid anchors. Beli comes to me. He's a small man, but that doesn't bother him. He looks me straight in the eye. "If you have no real friends over there, you must return here. That's an order." I don't know what to reply. And then the emotion tightens my throat, and I feel that if I open my mouth I'll start sobbing uncontrollably. We make our way towards your last resting place. Your female cousins, close or distant, strut like chickens with the designer handbags and Italian shoes they bought in Milan. Their mediocrity is inherently universal: human beings are everywhere the same. The crowd comes near to the place where your coffin will be deposited for all eternity. Suddenly, from high up on the little path descending towards the plot, I spot a tall silhouette striding along. I see that it's a woman, despite her almost hairless skull. She resembles a Buddhist monk, with her loose clothing that sweeps the ground. She has eyes only for me, and smiles from afar. Nervous, I look around me. No one seems to recognize her. Nor do I, but the closer she gets, the more her gestures, her hands, her skin and her soft smile seem familiar. Once she arrives, she throws herself on me like Beli threw himself on your coffin.

Selma, my best childhood friend, has just reappeared in my life like a fairy. The last time I saw her we were both twelve years old. I left her on a Friday, giving her an assignment for the weekend: to slap my boyfriend for what was doubtless a good reason, but one that escapes me today. All my pent-up emotions pour out in Selma's arms. I don't know if I should be mourning your death or celebrating my reunion with my best friend. In a typically Balkan confusion, I feel immense pain and immense joy simultaneously. Despite the yawning void that your death has left in my breast, life holds out the promise of continuity. Selma and I grew up in the shade of the same trees, and breathed the same exalted air of childhood. Together, we knew our first loves and our first pains, made our first gaffes and dreamed the first dreams of little girls who want to grow up too fast. Selma saw the first seeds sown in the fertile soil of my young years. Even if she wasn't there for their sprouting, she divined better than me the fruits they would produce. Finding her again, I understood that life is nothing more than an eternal attempt to reconstruct our childhoods. I also saw that the inalterable bond of our first friendships is the only torch that can cast light on the night that falls so swiftly when our first true bereavement is upon us. Thanks to Selma, I knew, for the first time in my adult life, a feeling of belonging and continuity, which gave me the strength and the desire to continue on my way. Selma is my Ariadne's thread.

THE VIRGIN
AND THE
CONCENTRATION
CAMP

THE DAY AFTER your death, a filmmaker friend asks me to think of a moment in my life that I could view forever on a screen. "Try," he tells me, "to come up with an image that would stop time and embody your idea of happiness." I think of my moments of joy with the Roma of Bišće Polje, of your reassuring paternal caresses, of the contagious laughter of little brother, of our clandestine trips across Europe, even of your dreams of Provence, but alas, none of these images last. And then childhood memories return, intact. I see myself again, ten or twelve years old, during one of Herzegovina's torrid summer nights, leaving the house in secret to steal figs and pomegranates from hateful Emma's garden. Someone spots us and shouts at us, waking the whole neighbourhood. Lights in the houses come on one after the other, like in cartoons, and we burst out laughing as we run, hair in the wind, pursuing the boundless happiness of our youth. The image remains graven in my mind, and there I find all the elements that make up my vision of childhood joy: play, light-heartedness, summer, friendship, the defiance of prohibitions, and fits of laughter. To be honest, this definition is still valid for me today.

My childhood's most vivid memories are all associated with light. The light pervading Mostar makes me think of a huge lantern suspended in the city's sky. Pure and exhilarating, it's that of Socrates' elation when he's trying to teach his disciples to see the world with newborn babies' eyes. Before the war, the inhabitants of Mostar applied this lesson to the letter: to live each day as if it were the last. Herzegovina's light embraces the Neretva's whispering, the cries of infants burnished by the sun, the fullness offered up by ripe and sugary fruit, all bathed in a splendour that fosters a shimmering state of awareness. My first vision of happiness was born of that light.

You only have to remove yourself a little from Mostar, however, to be faced with another reality, that of those enamoured of the Virgin, to see that faith too is a matter of light. Western Herzegovina belongs officially to Bosnia-Herzegovina, but you see the Croatian flag everywhere. The people feel deeply Catholic (and so Croatian), and refuse to think they might be Bosnian. The ethnic identity that is part and parcel of one's religious inclination is the dangerous equation that put an end to Yugoslav togetherness and its cultural mix. Thus, the grandiose idea of the European nation-state was given a strange twist in the Balkans: an ethnic group, a religion, a nation. Mama was born in Ljubuški, where a golden light similar to that favoured by Venetian painters filters through the stained-glass windows of Franciscan monasteries. The joy I harboured in my breast never touched the children in this primitive town. Every time I suggested some kind of prank, they spoke to me fearfully about the punishments that would ensue.

This arid region did not know the glory days of Tito's Yugoslavia, and its frequent droughts and floods caused people to be fearful and narrow. Its characteristic landscape, caught between mountains and the sea, has little to offer other than the medieval light that awakens one to faith and evokes a glorious past. The Franciscan museum on the way out of Ljubuški honours a history that goes back to antiquity, when the Illyrians were routed by the Romans. Archaeological digs have unearthed many valuable objects on the site of the Roman military camp in Gračine. The museum also contains a celebrated eleventh-century relic, the Humac plaque, with its description in Bosančica's ancient writing of the construction of the first church in the area. The region has been conquered many times, but only the Austro-Hungarian Empire has truly left its mark on the architecture. All the same, behind the lush vegetation, Ottoman islets do come into view, including the Žabljak mosque, poised on a hill that overlooks the town. When the Bosnian kingdom collapsed during the Ottoman conquest in 1479, tolerance reigned among a predominantly Catholic population, with a Muslim minority. However, the sixteenth century saw the ravages of the Ottomans, and many Catholic monasteries were burned. In the seventeenth century, the great Turkish traveller Evliya Çelebi related that he always avoided passing through Ljubuški, "because the enemy there is more than rebellious." The accumulation of small frustrations and great injustices generated in Ljubuški the notorious movement of the haïdouks, those rebel brigands who colonized the Croatian coast while launching raids against Ottoman caravans. There followed other uprisings, other empires, and finally the twentieth century, with its two world wars in the course of which the former Yugoslavia lost six hundred thousand of its children.

I remember grandfather describing with terror in his voice the chaos into which the country was plunged during those dark years when fellow countrymen fought, brother against brother, urged on by the huzzahs of European "friends" on one side or the other—Italians, Germans, or Russians, depending on the hazards of historical and strategic affinities. He also remembered the sound of German and Russian boots pounding the paving stones of the old city, and the hissing of pitchforks being thrust into straw in the search for Jews.

Ljubuški's inhabitants keep alive the memory of the five Franciscan monks, now Catholic martyrs, executed by Tito's partisans. When you ask the neighbourhood veterans, but also the younger generations, why the Franciscans were killed, they reply in the most natural way in the world that it's because they were from the same town as Andrija Artuković. The "Croatian Himmler," minister in the Nazis' puppet regime, managed to flee to the United States with a false passport. The communist version is that the executed Franciscans were supporters of Nazi ideology. And that is how, generation after generation, a toxic memory is passed on.

Mama is the youngest of seven children. Her first name is as Catholic as can be. The black sheep of the family, she was always drawn to the Virgin, with her milky skin and her irreproachable behaviour. It should be said that she was raised in a town where every house has its crucifix, and where rosary beads are to be heard clicking away behind the white lace masking the faces of pious women. And so until the age of reason I thought that Mama was a fervent Catholic. With her black hair cut short, her doe eyes, and innocent smile, she nevertheless grew up in the shadow of the dangerous Christian idea that happiness is not of this world. The notion of pleasure was never part of my education, and whenever she had the chance, Mama presented me with a depraved image of the body as something that ought to disgust us.

Before the war, we did not often go to Ljubuški, except to visit my grandmother, who was always on the brink of asphyxiation and could no longer talk normally: every one of her sentences was a long complaint. Mama inherited from her mother this practice of poisoning others with her hypochondria. You hated your wife's home town, and you cursed your employer the day he shipped you off you to this "lost hole." Projektant, the Mostar architectural firm, sent you to oversee the construction of a road and a water reservoir. You tried to persuade your supervisors of the uselessness of the project, arguing that all of West Herzegovina's roads lead right to heaven and that God has no need of infrastructure. What's more, you felt that this valley fostered foul ultranationalist seeds in its arid entrails. Despite all Tito's efforts, the idea of a multi-ethnic identity would never flourish on that soil.

Mama, apart from her cruel capacity to implant her words in your heart, represents the polar opposite of your personality, your dreams, and your aspirations. Her venom is so powerful that you compare her to those dangerous serpents that sleep under stones in the medieval fortress looking down on the valley. Still, you yourself are no less venomous. Often I hear you say that you regret your marriage to "a peasant." You even advance the theory according to which urban dwellers should never wed villagers. Every time you're angry with Mama, you threaten to "rescind her right" to live in the city. "Maya, my dear, listen to me. You can marry whoever you want, but not a peasant, you understand? They all have a foul character!" And Mama retorts by reminding you that your idol, Tito, was himself a peasant from Kumrovec. Bereft of arguments, and also because you're always looking for a pretext to drink, you apply yourself to drowning her "serpent's tongue" in alcohol. Still, I like Ljubuški. Before the war we never stayed there for more than one night because you didn't want me falling in love with this "small town life." But I like the region's abundant vegetation, the low shadows of the fig trees, the fair where the locals are always trying to convert the Roma to Catholicism, and, above all, half-deaf Uncle Alica, who smokes the tobacco he grows himself, between arguments over politics with his neighbours. A hardcore communist, he shouts out to whoever wants to hear that nationalists should be imprisoned and tortured, even though they make up the majority of his clients in the dusty workshop where he repairs typewriters. Alica was born two years after the end of the war, but that doesn't stop him from telling stories about his heroic participation, at Tito's side, in the battle of Sutjeska against the Nazis and their Italian, Bulgarian, and Croatian allies. In the 1970s a film was made about this bloody confrontation, with Richard Burton in the role of Tito. My uncle, who is convinced that he looks like Belmondo, swears he was approached to play an important role, but, being too busy, had to politely decline.

Uncle Alica and Aunt Dubravka are brother and sister, but they declared ideological war before the beginning of the Yugoslav conflict. Dubravka, a strong believer, behaves like those Asian women who think they hold exclusive rights over all members of the family. She authorizes herself on a regular basis to invade her brother's workshop and to try to turn him away from communism. Alica, frightened by her words, bursts into the main street and cries: "Save me from this witch who's poisoning me with her religious potion!" Dubravka, in turn, gets angry and casts spells on him under her breath, predicting that soon his communist friends will turn on him. When the war broke out, Croatian soldiers came looking for uncle to take him to a concentration camp. His communist friends, who had from one day to the next turned into pious Catholics, observed in silence, hidden behind the lace covering their windows, the humiliation of their comrade, a Muslim who didn't want to be one.

I remember one morning, some years before the war. We are in Ljubuški to visit, as usual, the grandmother who says she is ready to depart for the other world. Wakened by a cock's crowing, I open the door of my room, and am immediately thrown backwards by Herzegovina's blinding light, so often described by poets and prophets. Seeing the expression of bliss on my face, you shake me as if to protect me from grave danger: "The sun is a huge, bright star that gives life. But if you look at it directly, it can make you blind." You fear that I'll develop a taste for hallucination, like other inhabitants of this godforsaken place: "You slept a lot. You heard my voice. You jumped out of bed and ran towards the light. You only looked at the sun for a second, but when it's at its height, especially when you've just awakened, you have to beware: it will not take long for the Virgin to appear."

The official story dates from 1981, when the Virgin Mary apparently appeared to six young Croats. From that day to this, the church authorities, both local and international, have tried to pass final judgment on the subject, to determine whether the appearances are genuine or not. You're then a respected professional working for the architectural firm Projektant, and the State sends you out on frequent missions to bring water and electricity to remote villages. There are many, and you don't especially like them because, you say, prehistoric people live there. You don't like the stagnant memories of men and stones that impede the flow of life. Stone and flesh are always confused in the Balkans. While the West, since the Enlightenment, has tried to put its finger on the elusive spot where consciousness intersects with matter, in the mysterious depths of the Balkan mind the body confronts matter directly, bypassing consciousness. Eastern Europe's mythology is full of walled enclosures, and even mothers who stubbornly persist in breastfeeding children entrapped in stone. *The Bridge on the Drina,* by Ivo Andrić, begins with twins walled up alive in the arch of a bridge, beneath which the blood and tears of poor people who cannot grasp the meaning of what oppresses them has flowed for centuries.

The Balkans are a multiplicity of viewpoints, and their tragedy consists in the desire of some to have the last word, absolutely, in relation to the others. And so alongside the official story of the Virgin Mary's appearance, there is also one that your photographer friend, Perica, told you and that you related to me in turn, claiming it was all a hoax designed to attract people from around the world to these remote parts, and, in so doing, to stimulate the local economy.

One day, during one of your distant expeditions at the wheel of your Russian Niva, along with Perica, whom you call the Blabbermouth, you arrive in Medjugorje. It's then a lost town in the back of beyond, in the hills between Mostar and Ljubuški, without paved roads, water, or electricity. Here and there a few old stone houses are nestled between two hills, and you wonder, looking at them, how their occupants are able to survive. "It's their unshakeable faith in the Virgin that explains their survival," asserts Perica, who, seeing the look in your eye, adds, "Without the most basic comforts, under this blinding sun, even the most hardened communist begins to believe."

It's 1981. Tito's death has shaken to its foundations the fragile underpinnings of the Great Socialist Federation, and an economic crisis is in full swing. The faithful's enthusiasm for Medjugorje grows, and the news spreads beyond the Yugoslav borders. Pious Italians are the first to flock to the spot, but Americans, and even Australians, soon arrive to swell their numbers. The little village quickly becomes one of the most popular Catholic pilgrimage destinations in the world, and thanks to the sudden influx of foreign gifts, its infrastructure now resembles that of a rich Los Angeles neighbourhood.

More than forty million pilgrims have visited "The Oasis of Peace" in Medjugorje. Pope John Paul II urged believers to go there, explaining the Vatican authorities' institutional silence by the fact that they are forbidden to pronounce on the genuineness of this kind of phenomenon during the clairvoyants' lives. On the secular side, after studies were conducted, no scientific authority determined that the six clairvoyants were mentally unstable. In the long run, none of that is of any importance. What matters is that the phenomenon produced an unshakable faith in thousands of pilgrims. Where to draw the line between fiction and reality, between faith and reason, especially in countries harbouring all illusions, all beliefs, and all hopes? This back of beyond with no water or electricity was transformed, thanks to faith, into a prosperous region. I've been there often, and more than once I've experienced a contradictory feeling of mystical communion and indignant exasperation. It's almost a physical law in the Balkans: good and evil, truth and lies, walk step in step. In Medjugorje I saw some unleashing their hatred in the face of imposture, while others sang a hymn of divine love. I also saw paraplegics walk, the lonely find love, and the poor become rich.

The Virgin continued her visits to Medjugorje while the war was wreaking havoc only thirty kilometres away. But if we think about it, Yugoslavia's short life has a lot in common with the Virgin's appearances. As long as you believed in it, it existed. One day perhaps, the Virgin will reappear to children tired of wars and territories, to a generation thirsting for love and sharing and immune to the poison of demagogues, to daughters and sons ashamed of their parents, who chose silence and consented to massacre while the Virgin was bringing them a message of peace.

In *Christ Stopped at Eboli*, Carlo Levi paints an accurate picture of life for poor peasants everywhere. Forgotten by the State and by all the men in power, these poor devils, wherever they may be, are never true citizens. Left behind in a pagan bubble that does not exclude piety, whether they come from the remote corners of Herzegovina or the arid lands of Matera, they have in common a life of suffering, of poverty, and of resignation. "The peasants were coming up the road with their animals and surging into their houses as they did every evening, with the monotony of a ceaseless tide, in a dark, mysterious world of their own, where there was no hope." In this monotone world, they are the sun and the rain, the beast and the plough, the bee and the fruit, the incessant labour, and, at times, the revolt. The Hajduks chased off the Ottoman caravans, the brigands in Lévi's book defended another Italy, the *guajiros* aided the revolutionary Cubans.

Lévi has Caruso, a fierce band chief, say: "If the world had only one enormous heart, I'd tear it out." This suppressed appetite has been smouldering for centuries in the Balkans, and it is common to all poor people, regardless of their ethnic or religious loyalties. Descendants of brigands and Hadjuks in the mountains of Western Herzegovina visited by the Virgin, the peasants of Podveležje who pray to Allah, or the inhabitants of rural Bosnia who prostrate themselves before popes with long beards, all have, buried within themselves, a desire for justice and a better life. From this desire may come the needed revolutions or blind massacres. All wars require the poor, and their lack of culture enables demagogues to recruit them, century after century, with vague promises. "*Ser cultos para ser libres.*" To educate the peasants and the poor is Fidel's true badge of honour. Is that the reason you systematically passed on to me your obsession with the Cuban Revolution?

CHRONICLE OF
A MURDERED CITY

Dᴜʀɪɴɢ certain twilights that bear down on Montreal's roofs, I feel the weight of four thousand years of memory. "In lovely blue the steeple blossoms with its metal roof," sings Hölderlin, in love with his native land. But when you have no land, what to sing? When I close my eyes in bed, I see the earth spinning in its eternal night, waiting for I know not what. Another question then comes to mind: where to go in the world when you've been all the way around it? In these morose moments I feel myself, like my planet, to be adrift with no goal. I am simply there, suspended in life, for no reason.

Visiting my childhood city along with Selma, I wander happily through the streets, despite the war's ghosts, taking in people and nature. In my memories, the steep hills surrounding Mostar weren't so high. I'm surprised to see I was born in a valley with no horizon. This landscape lends itself to the proliferation of different ways of thinking, distressing and difficult to grasp, on both sides of the great river that runs through and divides the land. In the old town, partly destroyed then rebuilt thanks to international aid, the Turks have set up their consulate on the main street, which leads towards Stari Most. Their defunct empire has left its mark on monuments recalling the architecture of Istanbul. It has also left its mark on local customs. The Bosnians have embraced this otherness to such a degree that, over the centuries, they have become true Asians, submitting in silence to the fate decreed them because *God wanted it thus.*

Selma and I decide to go to Istanbul to seek out the origins of this side of ourselves. I find with astonishment that Bosnian cities are an echo of old Constantinople. It's only in walking by the shores of the Bosphorus that one sees the degree to which the city of cities' thorny rosebushes have put down such deep roots in the Balkans. I see in Istanbul the same gardens of lilac and jasmine, the same fountains, the same characters from another century, the same sadness in their eyes. Not far from the Sultanahmet neighbourhood, where Saint Sophia casts shadows over the sublime Blue Mosque, the words of Orhan Pamuk resonate in my ears: "I spent my life in Istanbul, on the European shore, in houses giving onto the other shore, Asia. Living near the water, seeing the shore opposite me, the other continent, reminded me constantly of my place in the world, and that was good. And then one day they built a bridge joining the two banks of the Bosphorus. When I climbed onto this bridge and looked at the landscape, I understood that it was even better, even more beautiful to see the two banks at the same time. I understood that it was best to be a bridge between two shores. To address two shores without belonging wholeheartedly to one or the other revealed the most beautiful of landscapes."

Unlike the Turks, the Bosnians do not have, geographically, one foot in Asia and the other in Europe. Still, many of them feel as Asian as people in Istanbul, and as western as the Viennese. They cherish their monuments, which the barbarians destroy periodically, but that they raise up again, out of pride and defiance. They embody multiplicity, that which allows them to claim a Turkish, Slav, and occidental heritage. They have learned that it is not compulsory, in an era of

Manichaeisms and archaic fears, to wall in a territory behind the frontiers of an arbitrary, because one-dimensional, identity. To walk through Istanbul in the company of Selma is to become intoxicated with the awareness that something very familiar is afloat in the city's air, and also flowing in our veins. That something is ancient, and bears along with it primordial emanations, tales of grandiose lives, vanished empires, forgotten loves. The old stone gives off this melancholy that also wells up, at times, from the paving stones of Sarajevo and Mostar, following me as far as America. The Turks call *hüzün* that Asian spleen I must have inherited from my Ottoman ancestors.

Back in Mostar after this exhilarating trip, I notice on one of the "facades of shame," the one that borders the famous boulevard that marks the place where the most murderous combats took place, that Coca-Cola has had the last word. An enormous canvas has been hung by the multinational's publicity department to hide the traces of war, and to promote their miraculous potion. *Podjelite dobar asjećaj!* ("Share good feelings!") As if Coca-Cola were the only ones capable of uniting the two banks of a city that was, once, the most multi-ethnic in Europe. Today, *favelas*, like a cancer, are gnawing away at the left bank. Lacking space, the Bosnians no longer know where to go. On the Croatian side, an ultranationalist megalomania is in vogue. Encouraged by crafty politicians, the new Croatian arrivals pouring into the neighbouring villages have rebaptized the streets with names whose origins they do not even know: "King Tvrtko Street," "Queen Catherine Boulevard," "Princess Svjetlana Street." I ask some passersby to tell me who this King Trtkvo, this Queen Catherine, this Princess Svjetlana are. No one knows. "What counts," one of them says, "is that the new streets bear our names." You have to replace the old names, those of the Yugoslav partisans—whether they be Serb, Bosnian, or Croatian. You have to excise the memory of those who fought fascism, since fascism has just been revived. It's not even shameful to give streets the names of generals who fought side by side with the Nazis anymore, because in the end, say some of the newly arrived, it's a matter of "celebrating our history."

Elsewhere, if someone dared to name a boulevard in homage to a Nazi or a collaborator, civilized Europe would be scandalized, and would seek out the guilty. But in the Balkans it's normal. On the Neretva's other bank, the main artery of Mostar-East bears the name of Josip Broz Tito. The Bosnians, and especially the *Mostarci*, are still nostalgic for the Yugoslav past, when everyone lived together. But Mostar is today a city torn apart. It's also the one that possesses the most steel-reinforced doors per capita. I can protect myself from my neighbour, or shoot at him and shut myself in my house: no one will be able to beat down my door. The people in Mostar have learned to beware of their neighbours, and the time when the city's doors and windows were always wide open seems very far off. In appearance, traffic between the two shores is free, but an invisible frontier divides the city. The cars and passersby circulate with no problem, yes, but the tension persists. It is there, in every gaze, in every accent, in every word. The Catholics have installed an enormous cross that looks down on the entire city, as if to demonstrate that they have the last word. The Croatian flag is everywhere. But Mostar is not Croatia: the city belongs absolutely to Bosnia-Herzegovina, but no one would dare to say so, for fear of breaking the truce or being beaten to death.

At the bistro below our building, I order a coffee to go. The server makes a mistake and brings it in a cup. Forced to remain at the counter, I engage him in conversation, praising his coffee. "What brand is it?" He doesn't know. What he knows is that the Phoenix serves the same.

"You know where it is?"

"Phoenix? In the United States . . ."

"No, it's the other corner bar, two streets away."

He deduces from my ignorance that I come from the west bank, on "*their*" side, I can see it in his suddenly scornful eyes. The coffee is bitter, and I can't finish it. I pursue the conversation so as not to show my unease. From hostility, he shifts to seduction. As he's romancing me, without knowing why I suddenly feel disgusted with myself. I think it's because the coffee tastes of hatred. His or mine? Feeling detested incites you to detest. It's buried, like a pulse, hard to put into words. And to think I was born in a city that so prided itself on its diversity! This past seems much more interesting than the future being shaped by the nationalists, who only classify, differentiate, divide. To paraphrase Predrag Matvejević, Mostar's great essayist, the Balkan man, today, is like a spider weaving a web about him that isolates him from the world.

A bit later, I go into a shoe-repair shop to have my purse fixed. Recognizing my accent, the man sends me curtly over "to the left side." Because it's on the left side of the river that the former city-dwellers, who are today besieged, live. He is vile. He looks me up and down with disgust. I wonder how the city-dwellers who refused to leave during the war were able to sleep, when at any moment they might be killed or sent off to a camp. The best way to escape this madness is perhaps to talk only to foreigners? But not to those from countries nearby. Russia, France, Italy, Germany, have chosen their friends according to their religious orientation, history, and economic interests. Only China seems far enough away to escape these "dangerous liaisons." I catch sight of *The Dragon's Cave*, the new Chinese store. "They're everywhere, those Chinks!" grumbles a stooped centenarian, dragging along a bag that's too heavy for him.

The owner of the store is sitting by the door of his empty shop. An idle taxi driver is engaging him in conversation. "They say there are a lot of Chinese in Sarajevo . . ." The shopkeeper, meditative, doesn't reply. Does he speak the language? A Roma beggar passes by. When he sees the child, the Chinese man shows that he knows at least a few words of Serbo-Croatian: "Get out of here, you little fucking thief!" He's learned the Balkan rule: you only emerge from your daydreams to insult others. I turn on my heels. It seems the spores of hatred and suspicion are saturating the air of all Slavic countries. Every gesture is scrutinized, every word has two meanings, every look is imbued with fear and scorn. Everyone thinks he's better than the other. Everyone is more intelligent than his neighbour. In the endlessly incomplete settling of scores, where Roman Catholicism tries to prevail over Byzantine Orthodoxy and both act together to drive out Islam, you don't know where to turn to find a bit of relief.

Saturday. It's nine o'clock in the morning, and it's already hot. I'm sipping a coffee in the same bistro below my building. Two deputy ministers are discussing the state of the country. They're exasperated. One is Bosnian, the other is Croatian. In veiled terms, their voices low, they are talking about the next war. Because there will be one, of that they're certain. After a few insults addressed to their respective religions, Islam and Catholicism, they move on to the dichotomy between peasants and city-dwellers. They themselves were born right here, where, on the site of this bistro, there was once a magnificent garden where the home of nobles descended from sultans rose up. These "barbarians" have never heard of Mišo Marić, the poet! And they don't know anything about the most famous choir in the city, the Mostarske Kiše (whose name means, literally, "the rains of Mostar") either. "Do you know what they answer when I ask them if they know our choir? They ask me at what time of the year those rains fall!"

They chortle quietly, but the frustration can be read on their faces. The valley of the Neretva has become a bitter valley, despite the trees and fruits that grow there still. Today, two cultures try to live together, but their fancied superiority prevents each of them from seeing clearly how to do it. The city-dwellers can't abide the country folk who now rule them;

because most of them are in exile, it's the peasants who win the vote. "What interests them is paved streets and concrete. They all want to come to our beautiful city," remarks the Bosnian minister. It's always been like that here. There's no better man than a *Mostarac*, and his city is the most beautiful in the world. I watch the two men, and I'm overwhelmed by sadness, because they make me think of you: they're surviving thanks to their memories.

The Mostar high school, a magnificent building inherited from the Austro-Hungarian Empire, was almost demolished by missiles during the war. As it's on the dividing line, it's been entirely restored by the international community. Politicians on both sides of the Neretva claim that this is a perfect example of the coexistence of cultures in Mostar and of the new values the city wants to adopt. And yet the school has two entrances: one for Bosnians, the other for Croatians. The two groups of students do not interact, they do not have the same teachers, and they do not learn the same subject matter. In the unbridled demand for "the right to be different," each persists in demonstrating that everything *is* different: the language and history, of course, but also geography, chemistry, physics, mathematics. The country is like Babel the day after the divine punishment. In this absolute chaos, no one speaks the same language anymore. Education, the parliament, the media, justice, telecommunications, electricity—all is dual, and each shore lives according to its own laws.

On the way out of Mostar, somewhere between Metković and Počitelj, a sign proclaims: "To each his republic!" as if territorial constraints were an illusion, as if the Balkan peninsula were as vast as the Siberian plains or the Canadian far north. The Catholic Croats no longer want to be part of Bosnia-Herzegovina, but to be annexed by Croatia. The Serbs of Bosnia, for their part, want to rejoin Serbia. "And us, we have nowhere to go," say the Bosnians. Generations pass, but the hate remains. "Mad dogs, an inferior race, Turkish bastards":

that is what the Croats call the Bosnians. The latter are no more generous: "Fascists, peasants, thieves, criminals!" As for the Serbian population of Herzegovina, it is a minority within the minority, and so triply discriminated against, and tragically silent.

In the former military barracks, the Muslims, financed by King Fahd of Saudi Arabia, have built a mosque. It's on the left bank, but the muezzin's voice doesn't stop at the Neretva. The Catholics on the right bank, and also some lay Muslims have complained. They've asked that the speakers' volume be lowered, as they wake the whole city before dawn. The Islamists refuse to listen. The ultra-Catholics have reacted by erecting their enormous concrete cross on the hill overlooking the city. At night, it's so brightly lit you can see it from everywhere. Fortunately, Mount Velež, which dominates the valley, is there to mock men's madness with its thousand metres of elevation.

I decide to pay a visit to one of your childhood friends. I want to ask her about your life before us, to learn about your youthful dreams. Facing the Karabeg mosque, Sada has transformed her garage into a stifling pottery studio. Cigarettes have made her voice hoarse and almost masculine, but she doesn't care: like that, she says, she resembles Jeanne Moreau, her favourite actress. Sada learned pottery very young, not suspecting that this pastime would one day serve to support her whole family. Her mother, a curiously perky eighty-year-old, taught her everything, but has never succeeded in poisoning her mind with her religious convictions. More than forty years ago, Sada's mother brought to Mostar the Jehovah's Witnesses' strange doctrine. When she saw her daughter was ready to sacrifice her life for the Beatles, she prayed under her breath for her soul, lost in the netherworld of rock and roll. In vain: Sada became an atheist. *Pušim ko Turćin*, she smokes like a Turk and spouts smoke like a dragon while forming a vase: "You see, the Turks left us the worst poisons in the world: religion and the cigarette." Anger has transmuted into ulcers in her body, and her eyes spark with bitterness and disappointment. "The war dealt me one blow after the other. I don't know how I'm still alive. My whole generation is sleeping peacefully in the Sutina cemetery. I'll be joining them soon . . ."

When the war broke out, Sada fled Mostar with her family and, like us, found refuge in Switzerland. But her husband, a *Mostarac* who was even more insanely nostalgic than you, finally refused political asylum and repatriated his whole family. Sada thought it was a good decision because "you had to go back and defy the enemies and rebuild the city." Except she didn't suspect that the "enemies" were going to be her own people. Sada comes from a lay Muslim family. She grew up beside a mosque, but this monument represented for her a cultural, not a spiritual heritage. Sanja, her only daughter, grew up in Switzerland and was appalled when her parents forced her to leave her friends and return to the country of her birth. In Mostar the young woman, having lost all her points of reference, took refuge in transcendental meditation and marijuana. Then one day Sanja decided to marry a radicalized Muslim. For the wedding, the family of Sada's son-in-law forbade alcoholic drinks and "immodest" clothing. As Sada's favourite beverage was always Heineken, which she drinks though a straw and holds between her thighs just long enough to put a match to a Marlboro Light, she was furious, and refused to attend that "phony" marriage.

In Sultan Karabeg's mosque, the Wahhabis, whose fundamentalist movement originated in Saudi Arabia, took possession of both the furniture and the mentalities. "The fundamentalists have taken over the entire left bank!" Sada laments. When they hold their meetings, she lies in wait for them on her balcony and insults them liberally. "If you hadn't come along and paid them to go to the mosque, those poor peasants would never have come into the city!" For her, what's

stopping Mostar from becoming the cosmopolitan city it was
before the war is the invasion of a peasant mentality, no matter what the religion. "The species is everywhere the same.
All you have to do is to promise them a better life, and they're
happy to sell their mothers. Don't tell me their religion was
suppressed by communism. Communism was fine for them
as long as they could profit from it. But as soon as the State
coffers were empty, they started looking for another cash
cow!" On a torrid day (she swears it was forty-nine degrees
in the shade), Sada pulled the niqab off a woman who was
suffocating. She pulled out some of her hair as well. She says
she regrets nothing, not even her stay in prison.

I'd bought a summer dress in Vienna. As it was a bit long,
I gave it to Sada to alter, because this tiny woman can do
everything. She urged me to go and buy elastic and buttons
"on the other side," with the Croatians, because they always
have everything. "They're right, the Cathos, not to mix with
the rabble. I'm one, I'm Muslim, but what you see invading
our streets is a plague. Look at those peasants with their red
necks! Look at those boneheads being manipulated by the
first sect to come along! The worst is that they think they
know everything. What they don't know is that our Islam is
the lay Islam brought here by the Turks. We have nothing
to do with the Bedouins of Arabia and their obscurantism!"
When I point out that it's people's empty stomachs that impel
them to join the fundamentalists (the Wahhabis provide new
members with a tempting salary), Sada climbs the wall: "So
they sell their souls! I'd rather drink water and swallow air
than betray my principles!" Her foot tensed on the pedal of
her sewing machine, Sada guides my dress under the needle.
Something tells me this woman will not be able to endure for
much longer the weight of her own disillusionment.

Before going for a siesta, she tells me how to get to the
Croatian sewing store. "You'll see, they have everything, just
like the haute couture stores in Paris." To help me orient

myself, she chooses the National Bank building as a land-mark; "You know, the one with big frosted windows, facing the HIT commercial centre." But the National Bank and the HIT no longer exist. Having had the misfortune of finding themselves on the front line, the buildings were the target of two armies, and all that's left is a "ground zero." But in Sada's mind the two institutions are still standing. A few days before my leaving Mostar, Sanja calls me in tears to tell me that her mother didn't have the time to fix up my dress with the Croa-tian buttons. She had a heart attack and the doctors weren't able to do anything for her. At the funeral, I see her mother again, her daughter and her husband, each enclosed in his or her mental sarcophagus. The mother laments that her daugh-ter never wanted to become a Jehovah's Witness. It's too bad, she says, because "faith would have saved her from suffering." The daughter regrets that her mother did not respect the pre-cepts of Islam, "her true religion." As for the husband, worn down and plagued by remorse, he asks his wife to forgive him for having deprived her of a life in Switzerland, where she could have become Coco Chanel or Camille Claudel. On the cemetery wall, someone has written: "It's war: the city against the peasants."

Everyone seems to accept this explanation. Azra is a judge. She was a political refugee in Germany, but after a few years she had to return to Mostar. It was a matter of survival, she explains: "Homesickness and the grey German sky had made me depressive." Today, she too detests the "peasants." I ask her to elaborate, because I want to know how someone as educated as she is can simplify things to that point.

"I've nothing against them, but you understand, when you come to live in a new place, you adapt, you learn the rules of the game. The peasants, they don't change. They don't want to learn. They cling to their customs. The war forced them to come to the city, and they reproduce here what they knew back there. I understand why they are here: even if they wanted to, they couldn't go back because another peasant, another religion, has taken over their homes. The religions have learned how to manipulate those with no education. The Wahhabis give everyone 400 marks. That allows them to survive, and if the whole family contributes, to live quite well. On the other hand, they must go to the mosque and they have to vote for them. It's about the same for the Catholics. The fanatics govern the whole country, and to stay in power, they keep the masses illiterate and ignorant. Tito didn't want to educate all levels of the population. If he'd paid more attention to the deprived, none of this would have happened. But the fool just cared about the intellectuals. And when a storm breaks, it's the intellectuals who are the most cowardly!"

On weekends, the city is dead. There's not a cat in the street. Josip Jolé Musa, a former coach of the Velež football club who became a politician after the war, said one day that the country will be happy the day peasants of all ethnicities go back forever to their old mothers and their chicken coops. Before the conflict, young couples used to promenade every evening on the *corso*. The old people talk about it with nostalgia, because that's where the most beautiful couples in the city were formed. Today the place is a promenade for mad dogs. German shepherds, pit bulls, and boxers parade with their owners. The latter wear bracelets and gold chains, and all have the latest model telephone. Dog fighting is an illegal practise, but when two dogs meet and bark furiously, their owners exchange telephone numbers, and arrange a rendezvous. One of the hounds will lose a leg or two, but the owner of the other will win some "minutes" on his iPhone to call his fiancée in Norway or Sweden. "We wouldn't need dogs to let off steam if they'd let us finish the job. It's the international community that stops us from drawing a line once and for all," says Ivica in faltering English to a Chinese tourist. "*You're in the wrong country to be tourist. There are so many better places than this country!*"

Before leaving Bosnia-Herzegovina, I decide to visit my friend Marina who, strangely, wasn't at your funeral. The last time I saw her, we were thirteen. She's stayed thin, but today she has enormous breasts, false fingernails dotted with fake diamonds, and is wearing high heels despite the six-year-old girl clutching her. We throw ourselves into each other's arms and take a long time stemming the flow of our tears. Marina speaks first; "We should never have separated. If I'd gone with you, I'd have become like you." This compliment makes me uneasy. Marina sees it, and explains:

"You've really become yourself. You've had the chance to develop your talents. Today, you're an accomplished woman. Me, in this backwater, I have to do like everybody else to survive. You see, some good things came out of the war. Thanks to it, today you live in a modern, developed country. Every morning I have to fight with my mother-in-law, who wants me to get rid of my beautiful nails to dig in the dirt with her. What would you have become if you'd had to live with those peasants like me?"

That word again. What Marina doesn't know is that it's a very relative concept: with her artificial nails, her blinding, whitened smile, her dyed hair, her silicone breasts, her loud blouse, and her leather pants, someone might describe her as a "Balkan peasant." And she wants me to give thanks to the war!

"I would have developed my talents in my own country, too!"

"Don't be stupid. You don't know how lucky you are."

"You didn't know exile, dragging yourself from one country to another, without a penny and starving to death!"

"Don't exaggerate, Maya. We've had bad times, too. But they ended. Everything ends."

Juré, Marina's husband, has come to fetch us in his brand-new Mercedes convertible, which has just replaced his Porsche, too small for his needs. His hair is glued down with hair cream, his earrings are real diamonds, and his silly smile reveals several gold teeth matching the chain from which hangs an enormous cross. He invites us both to a chic Italian restaurant in Medjugorje. There, Juré tells me the story of their first meeting, which according to him was love at first sight, but unreciprocated. He instantly fell in love with Marina's milky skin and wasp waist while "my best friend," he tells me in a mocking tone, was more interested in his Mustang. Marina whispers in my ear, just loud enough for him to hear: "And why else would I have agreed to throw my life away with him? Besides, his third leg is pretty limp!" And she roars with laughter while her husband grinds his teeth and seems ready to hit her.

After the meal they decide to take me to visit their new house in another remote Herzegovina village. Marina's love for the land of Aphrodite has inspired her: it's an immense white villa that recalls those of the Greek islands. The house is adorned with furniture of the latest modern design that she herself went to pick out in Milan. Juré follows her around during the visit, as if to make sure his wife won't do something embarrassing. His telephone rings, he sees the number and answers in Italian, then changes languages, shifting to Croatian to spew his insults. He hangs up, apologizes, kisses his wife and mother, waves to me, and disappears in his car, trailing a cloud of dust behind him. Marina's mother-in-law, sitting in the living room, throws her a black look. Marina orders her to put on some clean clothes if she wants to sit on the white leather sofa that cost 3000 euros. The old lady leaves, slamming the door.

"That's it, go dig in the dirt!"

"Don't treat her like that, she's an old woman."

"She's mainly a snake who shoves her nose in everywhere."

"Tell me, all the wealth in this place where there's no industry, no factories, no substantial production . . . I don't understand. Every one's driving around in a luxury car. Where does the money come from?"

"From organized crime, drugs, stolen cars, alcohol, ciga-rettes. Since Tito is no longer around to hold the dogs on a leash, it's the law of the jungle here. Yugoslavia suffered two terrible earthquakes, one after the other: the fall of commu-nism and the rapid introduction of a rotten capitalism."

"You're an intelligent woman, why don't you ask for more from life?"

My friend adjusts her hair in the mirror.

"You know where my money comes from? My man is a big wheel in the drug trafficking that passes through Herze-govina on the way to Montenegro. He's being hounded by a Serbian Mafia that's been demanding a million dollars for five years. We get threats every day. You know why I painted the walls with whitewash? Because if they toss another bomb at the house, the drivers passing through this hole will maybe see what's happening and come to our aid."

"You're serious?"

"Yes. Last year, someone threw a bomb at the house. And as we're living 'behind God's suspenders,' as they say here, it took ten hours to get help. Here you can die with only the cicadas to sing you one last lullaby."

"To hear you talk, you'd think the country was still at war."

"In a way it is. In any case, a state of anarchy has been declared."

That night, Marina arranges a get-together with our child-hood friends at Ljubuški, my mother's village. Almost twenty years have passed since we last saw each other, but on catching sight of me, my friends cry out with joy. Some have lost hair, others have gained a few kilos, but I recognize their child-hood faces. They've done well: Tomislav has become a law-yer, Anté works in a bank, Igor has a luxury-car dealership, Milica is a schoolteacher, Anika works in an architect's office. Like Marina, they say they envy my life in Canada, my youth spent in Switzerland, my projects and my travels. They feel

stuck in a dysfunctional country that's very difficult to leave
to "live in the West." Fortunately, Igor says, they all have dual
nationality, Croatian and Bosnian, and if Croatia's integration
into the European Union leads to its entry into the Schengen
Area, it'll be a done deal. For them, it's shameful to belong to
Bosnia-Herzegovina, the only country in Europe with a Muslim majority. It's for this reason they so value their Croatian
passports.

They ask me questions about all the countries where I've
lived, but it's Cuba that interests them the most. Knowing how
much their pious parents hated communism, I remind them
of the Cubans' political affiliation. "Yes, but this is different. It's
an exotic communism." I change the subject. Marina smokes
a joint while counting the stars in the sky. Her head thrown
back in a comfortable bamboo armchair, she murmurs: "You
know, if you lived in this backwater, sooner or later the mentality would get to you . . ." A stranger joins us. Anté introduces him as the godfather of her first child. As soon as he
arrives, the man looks at me suspiciously. When the waitress
comes to take our order, I ask for a second coffee. I say "*kafa*,"
like the Bosnians. The man corrects me sententiously: "Here
we say *kava*. If you want to drink *kafa*, you have to go to the
Muslims, in Mostar." Furious, I leave, barely saying goodbye
to my old friends. Marina, who follows me, opens her car
door and shoves me inside for a series of reprimands:

"It's obvious that you don't live here anymore! Nationalist
remarks are second nature now, they're part of the collective
unconscious. You shouldn't pay them any mind. Don't you
see that this guy, like everyone in this hole, is still living in
the eighteenth century? Today, on the surface, they seem
a bit more civilized, but deep down they could just as easily want to stone you or burn you alive because of one word:
kafa. Nothing has ever really changed in the Balkans, Maya . . .
when are you going to get that through your head?"

A CENTURY
OF TORMENT

NIETZCHE was right. It's upon the death of those we love that they become for us a shining star. With the passing of time, I see that the only truths that count are those one feels in one's body. It's in my body that my lack of you—your laughter, your odour, your wrinkles and your hands—makes itself felt. I miss, physically, your presence, gentle and violent at the same time, like a tropical rainfall. There are many days when I'd like to make my way to your grave to feel you near me. But we are separated by seven thousand kilometres, and so I often spend the night on Google Earth looking for your cemetery.

Little brother turned thirty this year. He expressed the desire to seek out his family and childhood friends in Mostar, but deep down it was you he wanted to see again, just like Mama and me. All three of us went to gather around your grave, but I returned to it alone to talk to you and ask your advice. You sleep in Herzegovina's harsh aridity, surrounded by cypresses that cast shade over your grave, set down like a precious stone in the valley where the emerald Neretva has scooped out its path. I prefer to be alone to talk to you about the world and its torments, about this infernal century that has just ended. Because exactly one hundred years ago, on

June 28, 1914, in Sarajevo, Gavrilo Princip assassinated the heir to the Austro-Hungarian throne. His act was the pretext for the First World War, the cause for the disappearance, in Europe, of three empires: the Ottoman, the Austro-Hungarian, and the Russian. And that is how, after the massacre, the maps of Europe and the Middle East were redrawn in haste. One man, one idea, one act. The lit wick that exploded the barrel of gunpowder.

Sarajevo opened the century with blood, and closed it after the longest siege in the history of modern warfare: from April 5, 1992, to February 29, 1996. The number of civilians killed is estimated to be more than 100,000. The record for the number of shells to fall on the city in one day: 3,777. All of that, one hour's flight time from Paris, in the name of an ultranationalism just like all the others that are springing up like poisonous mushrooms all over Europe. The eternal return of the same. . . One wonders how to escape it. One never really does, even thousands of kilometres from one's native land. There are places and times where it's not good to be born. I think of all the uprooted to whom one repeats: "How lucky you were to escape!" I think of your sacrificed generation, and of all the others, and of all those graves. I think of those who survived but bear in their hearts the silence of graveyards and who get up every morning pretending nothing is wrong. I think of my friend Svjetlana. You remember her?

This gentle exile always seemed to me to be prey to a certain sadness, even if the true reasons for her melancholy eluded me for a long time. I knew she came from Sarajevo, and that she was, like most of those native to that city, the product of a mixed marriage. I knew she had one brother, and that her parents "died in time"; that is, before the war. Svjetlana and her husband, Dejan, like thousands of other inhabitants of Sarajevo, endured the martyrdom, but never lamented their fate. In many ways they reminded me of you, with their typically Slavic sense of derision. When I showed an interest in their lives during the war, they described their worst moments with stoic, at times surrealistic humour.

That is how they told me that, one October night in 1993, in the besieged city, while they were seated around their one meal of the day, a dish of rice they'd received through humanitarian aid, a sniper posted in the neighbouring hills targeted Svjetlana's head. It's to the complete works of Freud—Dejan, a philosopher and intellectual of the highest order, had refused to burn them for heat—that Svjetlana owes her life. The bullet lodged in the wall of piled up books, embedding itself in *Three Essays on Sexual Theory*. Dejan had his own theory regarding the sniper's act. The murderer, a neurotic who'd never been able to express his sexual urges, experienced, thanks to each of his victims, a long-distance orgasm.

Despite her sense of humour, Svjetlana continued to face, every night, her worst enemy. The war had left her a legacy of chronic insomnia, and despite all her Western and oriental medical treatments, her eyes refused to close on the world, as if they had to watch over her to forestall other catastrophes. This terrible handicap never hindered this strong woman from making her way. On her arrival in Quebec, she quickly learned French, got her degrees, and found employment as a social worker. Stylish, she matched her shoes to her handbags, and her jewellery to her belts, and when she passed through the doorway of the ministry where she worked no one could suspect her of having those sleepless nights.

One day, in the course of an innocent conversation, I learned that her twin brother—truly, our lives are full of them—had been declared missing with his wife ever since the war. Svjetlana assumed they had been murdered and tossed into a common grave. But without any tangible proof, even after almost twenty years, the fear of missing some sign from her brother had blocked her access to the land of dreams. Until the previous year, when one May day an international

human-rights organization left a message on her voicemail.
The tone of the message, which she listened to dozens of times
before answering, augured the worst. She called the person
responsible for the dossier, a clumsy German who attempted
feeble jokes in Bosnian to comfort her, even though Slavic
wit is harder to master than the language. He requested her
presence in Sarajevo to identify the remains the organization
took to be those of her brother and sister-in-law. When, for
the first time since the war, Svjetlana set foot on the soil of her
native land, she still hoped it wasn't her brother, even while
dreading the imminent dénouement of her family tragedy.
Hope and affliction in a single feeling, as it has always been
in the Balkans.

Thanks to the made-to-measure Swiss watch she'd given
him, Svjetlana immediately recognized her brother. A trained
architect, he'd asked for a watch band all in bronze, because,
Svjetlana remembers, her voice trembling, "He wanted it to
be made of indestructible material so that future archaeolo-
gists would be able to find what was left of a lost humanity." It
was in a country she no longer knew that she was finally able
to bury her brother and sister-in-law. Near the shattered skeleton of her adored twin, she placed the bronze watch. "How
could you bear that?" asked her colleagues, when she was
back in Montreal. "I expected it . . ." replied Svjetlana, clothed
once more in her armour. "How strong you are!" But what
else could she be? And what did it mean exactly, "not to be
strong?" To throw oneself from the Jacques Cartier Bridge?
She would never have had the courage. It's weakness that
makes us strong. People reason a lot about the misfortunes
of others, but the misfortune itself involves no reasoning. It
strikes when it strikes, that's all. You just have to learn to live
with it, try not to care about it. That's it, the legacy of the Balkans: knowing how to kiss off adversity.

One day, as they were living their lives, Svjetlana and
Dejan decided to usher in the summer by climbing to the top

of Mont Tremblant. In the middle of the climb, Svjetlana lost her balance and fainted. Taken to the hospital, she remained in a coma for seventeen long days. The doctors, unable to determine the cause of her illness, gave no prognosis. She could tip one way or the other. Time would determine the fate of Svjetlana's body, fragile and bruised from mourning. When, slowly coming back to herself, she saw her son's face bent over the bed, Svjetlana wept for the first time since the start of the war. To comfort her, her husband, as always, teased her:

"With all the tissues you're using to wipe away your tears, we're going to have to cut down every tree in Canada!"

"I may destroy the forests, but I'm going to stop the pharmaceutical industry from getting rich on my back."

During her reprieve from consciousness, who knows what battle Svjetlana had to wage with darkness? But once out of the coma, she was finally able to sleep.

I tell this story because you would have wanted to hear it. Svjetlana and Dejan were your friends as well. After the uprooting we all experienced, there weren't many options other than death or resilience. But you didn't much believe in resilience. You said that, in one way or another, all this suppressed suffering would rise to the surface one day in the form, for example, of mental or physical illness. While Sarajevo and the whole new country that is Bosnia-Herzegovina commemorate the assassination that marked the start of a bloody century, I, in my turn, at your grave, deliver my own long speeches. How to escape the wars, the stuttering history of the Balkans? Every generation in our lineage has been touched by war: my great-grandfather, my grandfather, you and I, we've all known its ravages. I cast my eyes over your cemetery where the graves are too thick on the ground. What's the point of all that, Nenad?

I have come to your grave to share my concerns with you, but I want above all to ask for your blessing. June 28 is also the birthday of the man in my life. He's Cuban, do I really have to say it, given you always knew I was going to marry one, and that I would live my life on an island? I cursed your prophecy the day I lost Jaime, that first great love of which I spoke, timidly, in my first book. He died in a stupid motor-cycle accident, when we had our lives and our love all before us. I stopped believing in everything then, especially in love, and I wanted nothing more to do with Cuba. I remember your frail silhouette when you came to meet me at the airport after Jaime's funeral. You wept with me, but you also told me that I could lose everything except my faith in love, the only reason to be human. "You must absolutely continue to believe in it. Your Cuban is waiting for you, there will be another one, you'll see." I don't understand why you insisted that I abso-lutely must marry a Cuban. "You'll understand later, when history proves this little country right, and you'll see your child born into a society that still has faith in man."

At the age of thirty-five I understand better. Leandro, my husband, was present at Jaime's funeral. Afterwards, he remained in the background, until my mourning passed. From Miami, he sent me a letter each year, in which he declared his love and his availability. Ten years passed, and I decided to give him a chance. I've never regretted it, because our love is entire and unconditional, even if there are moments when I drift into darkness. If we form a stable couple today, it's doubtless also because we share certain con-victions stemming from a socialist education. The certainty, notably, that life's meaning is to be found elsewhere than in a frantic quest for the accumulation of material goods. Despite the deep differences between our cultures, Latin and Slav, we have many things in common, including the memory of those cartoons that all children in socialist countries watched avidly, beginning with *Lolek and Bolek*.

I saw clearly that we formed an unusual couple when I told those near to me that I was going to spend my honeymoon in Santa Clara to visit Che's mausoleum. My friends said that spending a week in this polluted Cuban city, lost in the countryside, was a ludicrous idea. And yet it's there that I found the happiness of a young married woman relishing, for the first time since her childhood, something resembling a meaningful life. Everything suddenly became clear, especially the logic of my uniting with a Cuban, of marrying Leandro. And it's in the shadow of Che's statue, of whom he often in fact reminds me, that I dedicated to him *Cantique des méridiens*, my second collection of poetry.

Sitting at your grave, I remember your funeral, and the unbearable moment when your coffin was sealed into a bed of concrete, you who wanted to melt into the humus that nourished your roots. I think again of another of your prophecies, the one you'd enunciated, exiting in fury the Presbyterian church in Ottawa, that I would complete on my own the last station of Christ: the lowering into the tomb, the end and the beginning of everything. One hand on my stomach, the other on the handle of the parasol sheltering me from the Herzegovina sun, I whisper to you that I'm now ready to conceive a child, and on a coast. I now know that it won't be that of the Adriatic, but rather of the Caribbean. As I murmur, leaning over your grave, my most intimate secrets, the midday heat, the emotion, and my hunger, turn my head. I don't want to leave you, but life is calling out to me, there, on the opposite shore of the great sea, in Havana or Montreal, where I've decided to extend our line, far from the tormented Balkans.

The next day, coming out of the museum dedicated to the memory of the victims of Srebrenica, a sudden weakness makes me stagger, and I pass out. The cousin who's with me mocks my fragility: "What would you have done if you'd stayed here during the war, and if you'd had to defy the snipers every day to go and fetch drinking water?" I don't know. Before casting off, I return briefly to see Beli, your best surviving friend, to talk about your youth. He tells me again that you were a champion skirt chaser, and that you loved the Roma and alcohol more than anything. He also shows me a letter you'd sent him from Switzerland, in which you'd declared your intention to write a book in which you would refute the belief that Ulysses finally reached Ithaca. I recognize your handwriting: "After more than two decades spent wandering, Ulysses couldn't have returned home. It's impossible. He'd lost himself in all his elsewheres. What has to be established in order to correct the story, is that he had a twin brother who stayed behind, and that people confused them. Ulysses died of nostalgia, far from his native land."

Leaving my former country, it seems to me that the war in Yugoslavia had been nothing more than an extension of the social conflicts of feudal times, whose echo, muted for centuries, had found its voice at last, waking from their sleep the calamity and the carnage: famished peasants pitted against privileged city-dwellers. Except that this time the country folk won. "It's their moment of glory. We must let them be. Everything passes: both men and empires. What's unfortunate is that we're there for this moment," says Dejan, before going to give a course in Greek philosophy to his Québécois students. One day, he tells me, that when one of them asked: "Sir, what is it good for, philosophy?" he replied: "For putting adversity into perspective."

I leave behind me your marble grave, on which I've placed white roses. Why did I never offer you flowers when you were alive? Just before I board the plane for America, Mama informs me of the death of your twin brother. He couldn't bear your disappearance, and found no other way than to disappear himself to feel worthy of your fraternal pact. At the end of the journey, Ulysses and his brother would find each other at last on Ithaca's soil. "Perhaps, after all, one's true native land is not of this world," this fragile woman who always secretly believed in the appearances of the Virgin Mary tells me in a broken voice. I delay my departure to attend the uncle's funeral. I witness the same circus that attended your own: one part of the family wants a religious service, and the other, still communist and atheist, wants no part of it. The tiresome agitation of the living makes me want to withdraw into a contemplative order, and, above all, to never again see the Balkans. But this feeling doesn't last long, that I have learned. *Mostarghia* returns when I wake in the middle of the night, not knowing where, or who I am. And so I lapse, periodically, just like the man who shares my life, into what we call our "patriotic circle": in one corner of the house I watch again the films, the documentaries, and the archives of the war in Yugoslavia, and in the other my Cuban prefers to reread the history of the Cuban revolution, from the beginning to the present day, even if he knows it by heart. In the plane bearing me home to him, I think of the number of hours we spend trying to lend meaning to the events that marked the histories of our countries and our lives.

As we pass through a strong zone of turbulence over the Atlantic, I feel within me something I've never felt before: the physical desire to have a child. In this metal machine that's like a comma in the wide sky, I'm overwhelmed by emotion. I realize that the desire to be a mother is inseparable from this feeling of which we were so deprived during our long exile: that the world has meaning.

Soon after touching down in the New World, I'm reunited with the man of my life, with his *guérillero*'s shoulders and his long hair like Che's, with his angel's smile, and his macho air that sometimes has him laughing at himself. We tell each other that we want, together, to make this ultimate pledge of freedom: to conceive a new life far from morbid memories and murderous identities. In his arms I feel that you are bestowing a blessing on us, and on your prophecy being fulfilled. It's time to write a new story, in a language your granddaughter will choose. Because it's a baby girl that Léandro would like to have, an *ex-Yugoslavita* who will dance like a Cuban, who will throw tantrums worthy of characters in Dostoyevsky, and who will think herself a born acrobat, like so many other little Montrealers who, when winter is done, take possession of their city's parks with their failed pirouettes. It's the first day after Babel.

ABOUT THE AUTHOR

Born in Bosnia-Herzegovina, Maya Ombasic fled the war in the former Yugoslavia with her family. She completed secondary school as a refugee in Switzerland and immigrated to Canada in 1999. Ombasic holds a master's degree in philosophy, a doctorate in comparative literature, and a diploma in filmmaking.

Ombasic is the author of two books of poetry, a collection of short stories, a picaresque novel, and works of literary criticism. She has made documentary films about Cuba and the North African desert. Her auto-fictional memoir, *Mostarghia,* was published in Quebec and France, where it was awarded the 2017 Literature in Exile Prize, and was later translated into Spanish.

Maya Ombasic lives in Montreal and teaches philosophy at Cégep St-Laurent.

ABOUT THE TRANSLATOR

Donald Winkler is a translator of fiction, non-fiction, and poetry. He is a three-time winner of the Governor General's Literary Award for French to English translation. He lives in Montreal.